# Resurrection

## *The Origin and Goal of the Christian Life*

Frank J. Matera

**LITURGICAL PRESS**
Collegeville, Minnesota

www.litpress.org

Cover design by Stefan Killen Design. Cover photo © Thinkstock.

1     2     3     4     5     6     7     8     9

**Library of Congress Cataloging-in-Publication Data**

Matera, Frank J.
    Resurrection: the origin and goal of the christian life / Frank J. Matera.
        pages      cm
    Includes bibliographical references.
    ISBN 978-0-8146-4862-9 — ISBN 978-0-8146-4887-2 (ebook)
    1. Resurrection—Biblical teaching.    2. Jesus Christ—Resurrection—Biblical teaching.    I. Title.

BS2545.R47M38    2015
232'.5—dc23                                        2014023484

*David,*
*With gratitude for*
*our friendship.*
*Frank*

This book is dedicated to
the parishioners of St. Mary's Church
in Simsbury, Connecticut,
in whom I encounter the risen Christ every day.

# Contents

Preface    ix

Introduction    Why the Resurrection Matters    1

Chapter 1    The Witness of the Gospel Tradition Apart from
the Resurrection Narratives    19

Chapter 2    The Witness of the Resurrection Narratives    36

Chapter 3    The Witness of the Acts of the Apostles    64

Chapter 4    The Witness of the Pauline Tradition    83

Chapter 5    The Witness of Hebrews, 1 Peter, 1 John,
and Revelation    112

Conclusion    The Mystery of the Resurrection    134

Annotated Bibliography for Further Reading    143

Scripture Index    145

# Preface

My academic career began with a study of the passion narrative in the Gospel of Mark, and for several years thereafter I pursued the theology of the passion narratives in the other gospels as well. But at a certain point my interest turned to the theology of St. Paul, and it was then that I discovered the centrality of the resurrection in the Christian life. When I retired from my teaching post at the Catholic University of America to assume the pastorate of St. Mary's Church in Simsbury, I decided to focus my attention on the resurrection in the New Testament, given the importance of this topic for pastoral ministry. This book is the outcome of that decision. I have written it for a wider audience with the hope of inspiring a deeper hope in the resurrection among Christ's faithful people. This volume is dedicated to the parishioners of St. Mary's Parish in Simsbury whom I am privileged to serve. It is they who have helped me to see ever new dimensions of the resurrection through their strong Christian faith.

I express my gratitude to Christopher Begg, professor of Old Testament at the Catholic University of America, and to Ronald Witherup, the superior general of the Society of Saint-Sulpice, for their careful reading of this text and for the suggestions they made for improving it.

Frank J. Matera
Professor Emeritus, The Catholic University of America
Pastor, St. Mary's Church, Simsbury, Connecticut

# Why the Resurrection Matters

This is a book about the central mystery of the Christian faith: the resurrection of Jesus Christ from the dead and the hope his followers have for their own resurrection from the dead. It may seem strange that I am writing such a book. After all, if Jesus' resurrection from the dead is the central mystery of the Christian faith, what need is there to write a book about it? Do not believers already understand the central mystery of their faith? It is true that most believers understand, at least in some rudimentary fashion, that the resurrection is the event upon which their faith stands or falls. But it is also true that many are puzzled by this teaching, which is so central to their faith. After all, if one's immortal soul enters heaven after death, is there any need for a bodily resurrection from the dead? In other words, while many understand the importance of Jesus' resurrection for their faith, they are puzzled about the significance of this teaching for their lives.

The reason for this book, then, is *to explain as clearly as possible what the New Testament teaches about the resurrection of Jesus and of those who believe in him so that contemporary believers will have a better understanding of what is most central to their faith.* This is not an easy task, however, since the teaching of the New Testament on the resurrection is multifaceted and complex. For example, whereas the gospels tend to focus their attention on the stories of the empty tomb and the appearances of the risen Christ, the Acts of the Apostles turns its attention to the preaching of the early church on the resurrection. Paul, for his part, provides us with a profound theological reflection on the meaning of the resurrection for the life of those who believe in Christ. Most importantly, there is the added challenge that the resurrection is a *mystery* that can never be completely fathomed. Accordingly, even after we have summarized and described what the New Testament says about the resurrection, we will not have exhausted its meaning. That meaning can only be appropriated by faith and participation in the mystery itself. And even then, when we have participated in the mystery by our own resurrection from the dead, we will not have exhausted the meaning of the mystery.

In the rest of this chapter I will do three things. First, I will discuss why the resurrection *was* so important to the first Christians. Second, I will offer some reasons why the resurrection *remains* important for believers today. Finally, I will discuss the structure, method, and purpose of this work, which I have written for a wider audience than the academic community.

## Why the Resurrection Was Important

Anyone who reads the New Testament cannot help but notice the central place the resurrection of Jesus plays in these writings. All of the gospels end with accounts of the empty tomb and stories of the risen Lord who appears to his followers.[1] The central theme of the Acts of the Apostles is the witness of the early church to Jesus' resurrection. The Pauline letters are, for all practical purposes, a theology of the resurrection.[2] The same is true for Hebrews, the letters of Peter and John, and the book of Revelation, all of which testify to the importance of the resurrection, albeit in different ways. If we remove the topic of the resurrection from the writings of the New Testament, these writings make little or no sense. The story of Jesus as related in the gospels ends in failure and tragedy. The central theme of the Acts of the Apostles—the witness of the church to the resurrection—makes no sense; and the driving force of Paul's theology (the newness of life that believers enjoy in Christ) is false. So why was the resurrection so important to the early church? Why does it play such a central role in the New Testament writings?

### God's Vindication of Jesus

The first reason that the resurrection was so important to the early church can be stated in this way: *By raising Jesus from the dead, God vindicated Jesus' life and ministry.* To understand this, imagine how Jesus' followers would have responded if they did not believe God had raised him from the dead. They would have lost their faith in the one who proclaimed that the kingdom of God was making its appearance in his life and ministry. They would no longer have found his teaching convincing and enduring. Jesus' ministry and teaching were so intimately related to his understanding and trust in God that it is difficult to comprehend why his disciples would have remained faithful to him if God had not raised him from the dead.

Death is the defining moment in every person's life. It marks the end of life as we know it. Jesus' own death was no different, and it appeared to contradict all that he proclaimed. He was condemned by the religious leaders of his own people as someone who had led God's people astray. He was executed by the Roman authorities as a political insurgent, "the King of the Jews." His death by crucifixion was a scandal to his own disciples, who could not understand why he had to suffer and die if he was the Messiah. In a word, the first Christians were confronted with the scandal of the cross that their enemies would use against them for years to come: If Jesus was truly God's Anointed One, why did God allow his anointed to suffer and die in such a scandalous manner? Was Jesus, after all, a deceiver? Did he die under God's curse?[3]

It was the resurrection of Jesus from the dead that enabled his followers to move forward. By this powerful creative act, God vindicated Jesus as his Anointed One, the Messiah, the Son of God. It was the resurrection that convinced the first Christians that God had not abandoned Jesus after all but vindicated him by raising him from the dead. The Acts of the Apostles develops this theme of vindication in a series of sermons that Peter and Paul deliver, which I will discuss in chapter 3. But one example will suffice for now. In his sermon at Pentecost, Peter says to those assembled in Jerusalem, "this man, handed over to you according to the definite plan and foreknowledge of God, you crucified and killed by the hands of those outside the law. But God raised him up, having freed him from death, because it was impossible for him to be held in its power" (Acts 2:23-24). The contrast that Peter establishes between what the people did (crucified and killed Jesus) and what God has done (raised him from the dead) highlights the importance of the resurrection for the early church. The resurrection was God's vindication of Jesus. By raising Jesus from the dead, God justified Jesus. It now became clear in a way that it had not been before that Jesus was God's anointed agent who had inaugurated the kingdom of God. It now became clear that Jesus was the Messiah, the Son of God, the one whom God appointed as Savior and Lord of all.

### Jesus' Proclamation of the Kingdom of God

The second reason why the resurrection of Jesus was so important to the early church is closely related to the first and can be stated in this way: *The resurrection of Jesus from the dead confirmed his proclamation that the kingdom of God had made its appearance in his life and ministry.* Put negatively, if God had not raised Jesus from the dead, there would have been no reason to believe in his proclamation that God's rule was making its appearance in his ministry.

The Synoptic Gospels attest that the central content of Jesus' proclamation was the imminent appearance of God's rule (Mark 1:15). By healing the sick, casting out demons, raising the dead, and overcoming the chaotic forces of nature, Jesus demonstrated what he proclaimed: the kingdom of God was at hand. To be sure, the kingdom had not yet arrived in all of its power and glory. That would only happen with the glorious appearance of the Son of Man, with whom Jesus identified himself.[4] It was clear, however, from Jesus' preaching that he saw his ministry as the way in which God was inaugurating the kingdom in his ministry and that the consummation of all things was at hand.

Jesus' ignominious death on the cross, however, called into question his central proclamation. If he was truly the one through whom God was reasserting his rule over history and creation, why was he put to death as a messianic pretender? If Jesus was the one through whom God's kingdom was overcoming the rule of Satan, why did the powers of Sin and Death overcome God's Anointed One?[5] Was the kingdom of Satan more powerful than the kingdom of God that Jesus had proclaimed? And if Jesus was to return as the glorious Son of Man, whose return would inaugurate the kingdom in all of its power and glory, how could this occur if Jesus was dead?

Once again it was the resurrection of Jesus from the dead that enabled his disciples to reaffirm their faith in him. By raising him from the dead, God demonstrated in a powerful way that the kingdom of God had made its appearance in Jesus. The disciples' encounter with the risen Lord convinced them that the one who proclaimed the kingdom had now entered into the fullness of the kingdom he proclaimed. As the first to rise from the dead, Jesus was the first to enter into the fullness of the kingdom he announced, the new creation that God had established in the one whom Paul calls "the first-born from the dead" (Col 1:18).

Just as God vindicated Jesus by raising him from the dead, so God vindicated Jesus' proclamation about the kingdom of God by raising him from the dead. The early church learned that Jesus' proclamation of the kingdom was true because he had entered into the kingdom through his resurrection from the dead.

## *The Experience of the Spirit*

A third reason why the resurrection was so important for the early church can be stated in this way: *The resurrection of Jesus resulted in a profound experience of the Spirit within the early church.* Thus, even though the vast majority of early Christians had never known the earthly Jesus or encountered the risen Lord, they experienced the power of God's Spirit, which Jesus' resurrection gave to those who believed in him. This experience of the Spirit confirmed what they believed: that God had raised Jesus from the dead and enthroned him as Lord and Messiah. Three examples will illustrate what I mean.

First, on Pentecost God poured forth his Spirit upon the apostles in a dramatic fashion. In his explanation of how and why this took place, Peter draws a relationship between Jesus' resurrection and the Spirit: "This Jesus God raised up, and of that all of us are witnesses. Being therefore exalted at the right hand of God, and having received from the Father the promise of the Holy Spirit, he has poured out this that you both see and hear" (Acts 2:32-33). The sequence of events that Peter describes is as follows. First, God raised Jesus from the dead. Second, God exalted him at his right hand. Third, exalted at God's right hand, the risen Lord received the promised Holy Spirit, which he now pours out upon the church. The outpouring of God's Spirit upon those who believe in Christ, then, testifies that Jesus is risen and alive.

Second, in Romans 8:11 Paul assures the Roman Christians that "if the Spirit of him [namely God] who raised Jesus from the dead dwells in you, he who raised Christ from the dead [God] will give life to your mortal bodies also through his Spirit that dwells in you." For Paul and the Pauline churches, the experience of the Holy Spirit assured them that God would raise them from the dead just as God had raised Jesus from the dead. The Spirit, then, was more than the source of wondrous gifts within the church; it was the first install-ment toward resurrection life (2 Cor 1:22). The Spirit was the one with whom believers were sealed for the day of redemption (Eph 4:30), and the possession of the Spirit was the assurance of their resurrection from the dead. For inasmuch as believers had already received the gift of God's life-giving Spirit, the power of Death no longer ruled over their lives.

A third example occurs in Paul's letter to the Galatians. When trying to dissuade the Galatians from being circumcised, the apostle reminds them of the intense experience of the Spirit they received when they believed in the gospel he proclaimed to them. Accord-ingly, he asks the Galatians, "Well then, does God supply you with the Spirit and work miracles among you by your doing the works of the law, or by your believing what you heard?" (Gal 3:5). Paul's rhetorical question needs no answer since the Galatians were fully aware that they received the Spirit when they believed in the message of the gospel, long before they considered having themselves circumcised and doing the works of the Mosaic Law.

For the early Christians, then, the Spirit was the outcome of Jesus' resurrection from the dead and the assurance of their own resurrection from the dead. Without the resurrection, there would be no Spirit, and without the Spirit, there was no assurance of their resurrection from the dead. In addition to vindicating Jesus and his message, then, the resurrection provided believers with the gift of the Spirit, which assured them of their own resurrection from the dead.

### *The Fulfillment of Israel's Hope*

A fourth reason why the resurrection was so important to the early church can be stated in this way: *In light of Jesus' resurrection from the dead, the first Christians began to understand that the resurrection of the dead, which had begun in the Messiah, was the fulfillment of Israel's hope.* For example, toward the end of the Acts of the Apostles, Paul defends himself before the Jewish king, Agrippa. Having been accused of betraying the faith of his ancestors by preaching that God raised Jesus from the dead, Paul recounts his former zeal for his ancestral faith: "And now I stand here on trial on account of my hope in the *promise* made by God to our ancestors, a *promise* that our twelve tribes hope to attain, as they earnestly worship day and night. It is for this hope, your Excellency, that I am accused by Jews! *Why is it thought incredible by any of you that God raises the dead?*" (Acts 26:6-8).[6] As the italicized words indicate, Paul draws a connection between the promise God made to Israel and Jesus' resurrection from the dead.

On first reading, Paul's defense is rather puzzling since Israel's Scriptures do not say a great deal about resurrection from the dead.[7] Moreover, the promise or promises that God made to Israel tend to deal with the promise of the land, the promise of progeny, the promise that Israel will be a great nation, the promise of deliverance from exile, the promise of a savior king, an anointed figure, the Messiah. There is little, if any, promise of resurrection from the dead. But this is not how Paul, according to the Acts of the Apostles, interprets Israel's history.

In light of his call and conversion whereby he encountered the risen Lord, the apostle understands that all of the promises God made to Israel have found their fulfillment in the resurrection of the Messiah, which prefigures the resurrection of all who believe in him. And so Paul and the early church viewed the many promises God made to Israel as pointing to a single promise: resurrection from the dead. The promises God made to Abraham and his posterity find their deepest fulfillment in the risen Lord who makes all who believe in him children of Abraham, Isaac, and Jacob, no matter what their ethnic origin. The promise God made to David finds its fulfillment in the risen Messiah who now reigns eternally over the house of Jacob. God's promises to deliver Israel from bondage in Egypt and from exile in Babylon receive their full meaning in the resurrection of Christ, which delivers humanity from the ultimate bondage of Sin and Death that separate humanity from its Creator.

The resurrection of the Christ, then, was important to the first Christians because they understood that in the risen Christ God brought the promises made to Israel to fulfillment. Apart from the resurrection, no matter how noble Jesus' death, God's promises would not have been brought to completion.

### *The Community of Jesus' Disciples*

If God did not raise Jesus from the dead, Jesus could not have reconstituted his scattered flock. If God had not raised Jesus from the dead, there would be no church. The final reason the resurrection was so important to the early Christians, then, has to do with the church. The first Christians repeatedly testified that it was in virtue of the resurrection that they had been gathered into the community of the church—the community of Jesus' disciples. For example, in the Gospel of Mark, after telling his disciples that they will be scattered on account of his death, Jesus promises them that after he has been raised from the dead, he will go before them to Galilee (Mark 14:28). Then, after Jesus has been raised up, the angel at the tomb instructs the women to tell the disciples and Peter that Jesus is going ahead of them to Galilee, where they will see him just as he told them (16:7). In other words, the risen Lord goes ahead of his disciples—just as a shepherd leads his sheep—to reconstitute his scattered disciples as his church.

The gospels of Matthew, Luke, and John also testify to this. The Gospel of Matthew describes how the disciples gather at the mountain in Galilee, where the risen Lord commissions them to make disciples of all the nations by baptizing them in the name of the Father, the Son, and the Holy Spirit (Matt 28:16-20). At the end of the Gospel of Luke and at the beginning of the Acts of the Apostles, the risen Christ makes his disciples witnesses to his resurrection who must preach repentance for the forgiveness of sins, beginning in Jerusalem, Judea, Samaria, and to the ends of the earth (Luke 24:26-48; Acts 1:8). Finally, in the Gospel of John, the risen Lord appears to his disciples in Jerusalem and Galilee. In Jerusalem he breathes the Spirit upon them, granting them the power to forgive and retain sins (John 20:25), and in Galilee he restores Peter—who denied him three times—as the one who is to feed his flock and tend his sheep (John 21:15-19).

Although we traditionally think of Pentecost as the birth of the church, the appearance of the risen Lord to his disciples marks the beginning of the church inasmuch as Jesus reconstituted the community of his disciples by appearing to them as risen and alive. But if God had not raised Jesus from the dead, Jesus would not have been able to reconstitute his flock. It was in virtue of Jesus' resurrection from the dead, then, that the first Christians understood that the risen one reconstituted them as the community of his disciples—the church.

Paul's letters testify to the same reality. Throughout his letters the apostle refers to the community of disciples as the church, or the church of God, by which he means the assembly God has called into being through the saving death and resurrection of his Son. God chooses and elects people as members of the new (eschatological) congregation on the basis of Christ's death and resurrection. If God had not raised Jesus from the dead, there would be no church. But by raising the Son from the dead, the Father "creates" a congregation of believers that remains in continuity with the assembly of Israel, and yet is new.

One can easily think of other reasons why Jesus' resurrection from the dead was so important to the first Christians. Here, however, I have listed those I deem most important because they are seminal to Christian faith:

1. By the resurrection, God vindicated Jesus.
2. By the resurrection, God vindicated Jesus' central proclamation that the kingdom of God was making its appearance in his ministry.
3. Because of the resurrection, the first Christians experienced the power of God's own Spirit in their lives.
4. In the light of the resurrection, the first Christians understood that Jesus' resurrection from the dead was the fulfillment of Israel's hope.
5. By the resurrection, the scattered flock of Jesus was reconstituted as the church.

## Why the Resurrection Is Important

If the resurrection from the dead affected only Jesus, it has little to say to our lives today. But this is not the witness of the New Testament writings. The New Testament repeatedly testifies that Jesus' resurrection from the dead has profound implications for the lives of those who believe in him. Not only will they be raised from the dead but their present life is *already* being changed and transformed. Accordingly, Paul speaks of the "newness of life" (Rom 6:4) that believers presently experience in Christ, and the Gospel of John speaks of the "eternal life" that believers enjoy now, which assures them they will be raised up "on the last day" (John 6:54).

### The Foundation of Christian Faith

The resurrection of Jesus is the foundation of Christian faith; it is that without which Christianity is no longer Christianity. If we remove the resurrection from the Creed, the Creed loses its coherence. If we downplay the resurrection by saying that Jesus did not really rise from the dead, but rather his disciples believed in him anew despite his shameful death, there really is no basis for faith in the general resurrection of the dead of all believers. For, if Jesus was not raised, those who believe in him will not be raised from the dead. As important as Jesus' teaching is, it is not his teaching that is the essence of Christianity but his resurrection from the dead. Faith in Christ is not simply faith in his teaching; it is faith in God who raised him from the dead.

The incarnation and the resurrection are the two pillars on which Christianity stands.[8] If Jesus was not the incarnate Son of God, he could not save humanity from the powers of Sin and Death. If God did not raise Jesus from the dead, God will not raise from the dead those who believe in Jesus. Apart from the resurrection, there is no eternal life. Apart from the resurrection, Sin and Death are victorious. Like the incarnation, the resurrection from the dead assures us that it was God who acted in Jesus' life and death.

### God's Response to Sin and Death

Sin and Death are the two great enemies that threaten our life with God and with each other. By "Sin" I mean more than our daily sins; I mean that power of evil that, were it not for Christ, would control our lives. In Romans 5 Paul explains it this way: when humanity rebelled against God, the power of Sin entered into the world. With the appearance of Sin, St. Paul tells us, another power made its entry, namely, Death (Rom 5:12). Like Sin, Death is a power that, were it not for God's work in Christ, would dominate our lives. It is the last enemy, the enemy we cannot escape. It is the enemy that would cast us into absolute nothingness if it were not for God's act of a new creation in the resurrection of Jesus Christ.

God overcomes the powers of Sin and Death by the death and resurrection of Christ, which is a single redemptive event. It is not as though Christ atoned for our sins by his death on the cross and then God raised him up to prove that what happened on the cross was true. Rather, God brought about redemption through Christ's death and resurrection. This is why Paul writes of Christ, "It [righteousness] will be reckoned to us who believe in him who raised Jesus our Lord from the dead, who was *handed over to death for our trespasses and was raised for our justification*" (Rom 4:24-25). What God has done in Christ has two phases (death and resurrection) that form one event. Consequently, if we deny the resurrection, we deny what happened on the cross.

## *The Moral Life of the Christian*

Contemporary believers rarely appreciate the intimate relationship that exists between the resurrection and their moral or ethical life. Many Christians think of the moral life in terms of rules and regulations: what they must do and what they must avoid. But this view of the moral life is only partially correct and woefully inadequate. To be sure, there are things that believers must do and avoid. But the essence of the moral life is the new life—life in the Spirit—that makes the moral life possible. Those who believe in the risen Lord already have a foretaste of the resurrection that will be theirs through the experience of the Spirit they enjoy—the Spirit of God that has been mediated to them through Christ's resurrection.

In Romans, for example, Paul writes that in our baptism we were buried with Christ so that "we too might walk in newness of life" (Rom 6:4), which is the resurrection life that Christ already enjoys. In Colossians the apostle exhorts his audience to live in a way that corresponds to the new life that is theirs in Christ: "So if you have been raised with Christ, seek the things that are above, where Christ is, seated at the right hand of God. Set your minds on things that are above, not on things that are on earth, for you have died, and your life is hidden with Christ in God" (Col 3:1-3).

While the general resurrection of the dead is a future reality for which believers long and hope, the resurrection of Jesus Christ affects their lives even now. Inasmuch as Christians have been incorporated into the risen Lord through baptism, the power of Christ's resurrection has already changed and transformed their lives. Those who are in Christ enjoy the life of the risen Lord through the gift of the Spirit that *empowers* them to live a morally good life. The moral life of the believer, then, is not a mere matter of following rules and regulations. *The morally good life of the believer is life in the Spirit of the risen Lord, and it is this Spirit who makes it possible to do God's will.*

### The Source of Christian Hope

Christ's resurrection from the dead is the source of Christian hope since his resurrection is not an isolated event of the past but the beginning of the resurrection from the dead for all who live in him. Therefore, those who believe in the risen Christ hope for their own resurrection. Confident that God did not abandon his own Son to death, they are confident that God will not abandon those who conform themselves to the pattern of his Son. The hope that believers have, however, is not limited to their own future; it extends to the future of creation, as St. Paul explains:

> I consider that the sufferings of this present time are not worth comparing with the glory about to be revealed to us. For the creation waits with eager longing for the revealing of the children of God; for the creation was subjected to futility, not of its own will but by the will of the one who subjected it, in hope that the creation itself will be set free from its bondage to decay and will obtain the freedom of the glory of the children of God. (Rom 8:18-21)

The resurrection of those who are in Christ will inaugurate the redemption of creation, which has been subjected to futility because of human sin. Peter makes a similar point about the new creation that believers await: "But, in accordance with his promise, we wait for new heavens and a new earth, where righteousness is at home" (2 Pet 3:13). The promise to which Peter refers is Christ's second coming, which is made possible because Christ has been raised from the dead.

While Christian hope expresses itself in different ways, the source of this hope is Christ's resurrection, through which God has overcome the last and greatest enemy—Death. Without this hope that God will conquer Death, human hope is limited to this life only. This is why Paul writes, "If for this life only we have hoped in Christ, we are of all people most to be pitied" (1 Cor 15:19).

### The Mission of the Church

Although contemporary believers rarely avert to it, the resurrection is the impetus for the church's mission to preach the gospel to all the nations. The reason for this is simple: inasmuch as Christ's resurrection from the dead is the beginning of a new creation in which those who believe in Christ already participate through the gift of the Spirit, it is imperative for those who belong to this new creation to proclaim the gospel to others so that they too can enter God's new creation. To neglect to preach the gospel to others, then, is to abandon them to the old age of Sin and Death. It is a denial of what God has done in Christ. It foolishly affirms that all will be well *even if* the gospel of Christ's saving death and life-giving resurrection is not proclaimed to the world.

The Gospel of Matthew concludes with the risen Lord commissioning his disciples to go forth and make disciples of all the nations (28:19). The Gospel of Luke ends with the risen Lord instructing the eleven to preach repentance and the forgiveness of sins in his name to all the nations, beginning in Jerusalem (24:47). At the outset of the Acts of the Apostles, the risen Christ spends forty days with his apostles, appearing to them and showing them by many convincing proofs that he is truly risen and alive (1:3) so that they will be able to witness to his resurrection "in Jerusalem, in all Judea and Samaria, and to the ends of the earth" (1:8). The resurrection of Christ is the foundation of Paul's mission to the Gentiles. Having encountered the risen Christ on the road to Damascus, the great apostle understood that the purpose of this revelation was to make him the apostle to the nations: "But when God, who had set me apart before I was born and called me through his grace, was pleased to reveal his Son to me, *so that I might proclaim him among the Gentiles*, I did not confer with any human being" (Gal 1:15-16). Paul's conviction that God raised Jesus from the dead, then, became the impetus for him to preach the gospel of Christ's saving death and resurrection to the nations, since the resurrection of the Messiah implied that God's new creation had begun in the risen Christ.

To summarize, there are several reasons why Christ's resurrection is important to believers today. The resurrection is the foundation of Christian faith; it is that without which there is no gospel about God's victory over the powers of Sin and Death. As the gospel of God's victory over Sin and Death, the resurrection enables believers to live a morally good life since they are now empowered by the Spirit of their risen Lord. This Spirit is also their source of hope for their own resurrection and their impetus to proclaim the gospel to all the nations.

## The Structure, Method, and Purpose of This Work

The structure of this work, for the most part, follows the canonical order of the material of the New Testament. It begins with the witness of the four gospels. Next it considers the witness of the early church as found in the Acts of the Apostles. Then it turns to the Pauline letters before concluding with the witness of Hebrews, 1 Peter, 1 John, and the book of Revelation. Although this arrangement does not reflect the chronological order in which the material was written since most of the Pauline letters were written before the gospels and the Acts of the Apostles, it has the advantage of presenting the material in a way that moves from Jesus to the early church to the major witnesses of the early church: Paul, Peter, and John.

This study is essentially theological in nature rather than historical. This does not mean that historical data is irrelevant to the topic of the resurrection or that I ignore historical questions. I do not. For example, I begin with the Gospel of Mark rather than the Gospel of Matthew, even though Matthew appears first in the order of the canon, because I am convinced that Matthew and Luke made use of Mark in writing their gospels. Likewise, I distinguish between those Pauline letters whose authorship is not in dispute and those letters whose authorship is disputed in order to show how later letters (whether or not Paul wrote them) develop the tradition of earlier letters. I do not, however, engage in the important debate about the historicity of the resurrection. Consequently, this is not a work of apologetics that tries to show that Jesus was truly raised from the dead, that he appeared to his disciples and others, that the resurrection is not a fraud. Rather, I begin with the New Testament claim that God raised Jesus from the dead and that the risen one appeared to others who proclaimed what happened to them.

This work seeks to draw out the theological meaning of the text. What does the text claim about God and God's work in Christ? What does the text affirm about the new situation in which believers find themselves now that Christ has been raised from the dead? What are the implications of the resurrection for the life of those who believe in Christ?

This work is also *ecclesial* in nature. It is written for those who already believe and seek to deepen their understanding of their faith. Its purpose is to strengthen the community of believers. Others may read this work to see what Christians believe about the resurrection. I, however, have written this work from *within* the community of believers in which I stand. Its purpose is to hear anew the proclamation of the resurrection in a way that will strengthen the community of those who believe that God raised Jesus from the dead.

This work is structured in the following way. In chapter 1 we consider the witness of the gospel tradition to the resurrection apart from the resurrection narratives. Accordingly, this chapter deals with intimations of resurrection from the dead. These include accounts of Jesus raising the dead, his allusions to and his defense of the resurrection of the dead, and statements in which he anticipates that God will vindicate him by raising him from the dead. After considering these intimations of resurrection from the dead, in chapter 2 we deal with the gospel accounts of the empty tomb and the appearances of the risen Lord with a focus on their theological meaning.

In chapter 3 we consider the witness to the resurrection of the dead found in the Acts of the Apostles. We begin with the appearances of the risen Lord to the apostles and to Paul. Next, we examine the proclamation of the resurrection in the speeches of Peter and Paul.

After examining the proclamation of the early church as witnessed in Acts, in chapter 4 we turn our attention to the Pauline letters, which provide us with a profound theological reflection on the meaning of the resurrection. Here we consider Paul's encounter with the risen Lord, the creedal statements and hymns in his letters that refer to the resurrection, his insistence on the resurrection of the body, the role of the Spirit in the resurrection, the resurrection and the creation of the church, the resurrection and the life of the Christian, and the renewal of God's creation.

In chapter 5 we consider the witness of four other New Testament writings: Hebrews, 1 Peter, 1 John, and the book of Revelation.

Although these are diverse writings, their moral exhortations draw a relationship between the resurrection of Christ and of those who believe in him.

Finally we conclude with some theological reflections about the resurrection as a mystery, an act of God, the beginning of a new creation, and how it shapes the life of the believer and of the church.

The resurrection is the central teaching of Christianity—that without which there is no Christianity. It is my hope that this volume will help those who believe to enter more fully into this mystery and invite those who do not believe, or who have fallen away, to consider the central claim of the New Testament: *God raised Jesus from the dead.*

## Notes

1. The exception to this is the Gospel of Mark, the best manuscripts of which end with the story of the empty tomb. Later manuscripts, however, include stories of the appearances of the risen Lord.

2. Paul J. Achtemeier argues that resurrection is the central theme of Paul's theology ("The Continuing Quest for Coherence in St. Paul: An Experiment in Thought," in *Theology and Ethics in Paul and His Interpreters: Essays in Honor of Victor Paul Furnish*, ed. Eugene H. Lovering Jr. and Jerry L. Sumney, 132–45 [Nashville: Abingdon Press, 1996]).

3. The text of Deuteronomy 21:23 ("for anyone hung on a tree [that is, crucified] is under God's curse") suggests that one who is crucified is under God's curse. Paul alludes to this text in Galatians 3:13 ("Christ redeemed us from the curse of the law by becoming a curse for us—for it is written, 'Cursed is everyone who hangs on a tree'"), suggesting that those who opposed the early Christian movement argued that Jesus could not have been the Messiah since he had been crucified and so died under God's curse.

4. Jesus seems to have adopted the expression "the Son of Man" from Daniel 7, which speaks of a humanlike figure, "one like a son of man" (Dan 7:13), to whom God gives dominion, glory, and kingship (Dan 7:14) after a period of suffering and persecution. This expression allowed Jesus to

refer to himself in a way that pointed to his suffering and vindication as the Messiah: just as the one like a son of man in the book of Daniel was vindicated by God, so Jesus would be vindicated by God after his passion and death.

5. Throughout this book I capitalize "Sin" and "Death." In doing so, I am following the thought of St. Paul, who personifies Sin and Death as powers that rule over unredeemed humanity.

6. Italics in Scripture quotations have been added.

7. Belief in the resurrection of the dead appeared rather late in Israel's history. For the origins of this belief, see Christopher Bryan, *The Resurrection of the Messiah* (New York: Oxford University Press, 2011), 9–34; James H. Charlesworth, with C. D. Elledge, J. L. Crenshaw, H. Boers, and W.W. Willis Jr., *Resurrection: The Origin and Future of a Biblical Doctrine* (New York: T & T Clark, 2006); Geert Van Oyen and Tom Shepherd, eds., *Resurrection of the Dead: Biblical Traditions in Dialogue*, BETL 249 (Leuven: Peeters, 2012), 2–116.

8. Whereas the doctrine of the incarnation affirms that the eternal Word of God was made flesh in Jesus, the doctrine of the resurrection affirms that God vindicated Jesus by raising him from the dead. Both doctrines, from different vantage points, affirm that God was present and at work in Jesus.

# Chapter 1

# The Witness of the Gospel Tradition Apart from the Resurrection Narratives

Although the gospels are not the earliest documents of the New Testament, they are an important witness to some of the oldest traditions about the resurrection from the dead. For example, they recount stories of Jesus raising the dead, and they preserve sayings that give us insight into his understanding of the general resurrection of the dead, as well as his faith that God would vindicate his proclamation of the kingdom by raising him from the dead. In addition to these traditions, the gospels recount stories about the empty tomb and appearances of the risen Lord. Accordingly, the witness of the gospels to the resurrection is a good starting point, even though the gospels are not the earliest writings of the New Testament.

In this chapter I examine what the gospels proclaim about the resurrection from the dead, apart from the resurrection narratives. Then, in the next chapter, I consider the accounts of the empty tomb and the stories of the risen Lord's appearances. My aim is to highlight the theological meaning of these texts and events rather than evaluate or establish their historicity. Accordingly, in this and the next chapter I ask the following kinds of questions: When the gospels recount stories of Jesus raising the dead or anticipating his own resurrection from the dead, what are they saying about Jesus and his ministry? When the gospels report that the tomb was empty and the risen Lord appeared to his followers, what claims are the gospels making on us today?

## Intimations of Resurrection

The Gospel of Luke narrates an episode that points to Jesus' resurrection in an oblique way. In a story that is unique to his gospel, Luke recounts an episode in the life of the twelve-year-old Jesus who goes to Jerusalem with his parents for the feast of Passover and remains in the temple—his father's house—causing his parents to become distraught at the loss of their son. *After three days*, however, Mary and Joseph find the child in the temple, sitting in the midst of the teachers, listening and asking questions (2:46). While this episode foreshadows Jesus' ministry in Jerusalem when he will take possession of the temple and teach the people of Israel in his capacity as the messianic Son of God, the statement that the parents found the child in the temple *after three days* anticipates a far more important event: the third day when the distraught disciples will find Jesus risen from the dead.

The gospels of Matthew and Mark foreshadow Jesus' resurrection when they recount how Herod put John the Baptist to death. Both Matthew and Mark introduce the story with a report of Herod's reaction to Jesus' ministry. Hearing all that Jesus has been doing, Herod says of him, "John, whom I beheaded, has been raised" (Mark 6:16; cf. Matt 14:2). Herod's remark becomes the occasion for both evangelists to recount how Herod put John to death. Although the readers of both gospels eventually learn that John was Elijah who has returned to herald the coming of the Messiah, they know that Jesus is not the Baptist raised from the dead. Rather, the perceptive reader comprehends the irony of Herod's remark, which points to Jesus' resurrection.

The Gospel of John contains similar kinds of remarks. At the outset of his ministry, for example, Jesus goes to Jerusalem for the feast of Passover. While in the temple, he drives out the sheep and cattle and overturns the tables of the moneychangers, thereby disrupting the temple's commerce. When challenged to produce a sign that will explain why he does this, Jesus replies, "Destroy this temple, and in three days I will raise it up" (2:19). Although Jesus is talking about the temple that is his body, the Jews mistakenly think he is referring to the temple built by Herod the Great. It is at this point that the evangelist confides to the reader, "But he was speaking of the temple of his body. After he was raised from the dead, his disciples remembered that he had said this; and they believed the scripture and the word that Jesus had spoken" (2:21-22). Thus, while the evangelist concedes that nobody, including the disciples, understood Jesus' remark when it was spoken, he explains that after the resurrection they remembered and *understood* what Jesus had said.

Something similar happens in a series of "riddles" that Jesus tells the Jews while he is in Jerusalem for the feast of Tabernacles. Jesus says, "You will search for me, but you will not find me; and where I am, you cannot come" (7:34). Puzzled by this remark, the Jews ask, "Where does this man intend to go that we will not find him? Does he intend to go to the Dispersion among the Greeks and teach the Greeks?" (7:35). Next, Jesus pronounces a second riddle: "I am going away, and you will search for me, but you will die in your sin. Where I am going, you cannot come" (8:21). Again the Jews misunderstand Jesus, this time thinking that he intends to kill himself. Jesus pronounces a number of similar riddles in the farewell discourse that he gives to his disciples, and like the Jews the disciples do not understand (14:2-3, 19, 28; 16:5, 16). But by the end of the discourse, Jesus explains the meaning of these riddles and his disciples begin to comprehend: "I came from the Father and have come into the world; again, I am leaving the world and am going to the Father" (16:28). Although there is no mention of the resurrection of the dead in these texts, the resurrection is the key to understanding what Jesus means. Jesus, the incarnate Word whom the Father has sent into the world, will return to the Father by his saving death and life-giving resurrection.

There are other texts in the Johannine gospel that are more explicit. For example, when he explains why he has cured a man on the Sabbath, Jesus compares himself to a son who only does what he sees his father doing. Referring to God as his Father and to himself as God's Son, Jesus says that the Father loves the Son and shows him all that he does, affirming that "just as the Father raises the dead and gives them life, so also the Son gives life to whomever he wishes" (5:21). Then in an explicit reference to the general resurrection of the dead, Jesus affirms, "Do not be astonished at this; for the hour is coming when all who are in their graves will hear his voice and will come out—those who have done good, to the resurrection of life, and those who have done evil, to the resurrection of condemnation" (5:28-29). Although the audience does not understand what Jesus is saying at the time, after the resurrection it becomes clear. The same can be said for Jesus' good shepherd discourse when he proclaims, "For this reason the Father loves me, because I lay down my life in order to take it up again. No one takes it from me, but I lay it down of my own accord. I have power to lay it down, and I have power to take it up again" (10:17-18).When these words are spoken, the audience does not know that Jesus is referring to his resurrection from the dead, but when he rises from the dead they will understand.

The texts I have discussed in this section are *intimations* of Jesus' resurrection. They do not explicitly proclaim the resurrection; and people only understand their meaning after Jesus has been raised from the dead. All of them, however, point to the climax of the gospel narrative, Jesus' resurrection from the dead.

## Raising the Dead

In addition to preserving stories and sayings that intimate the resurrection of the dead, the gospels recount stories of Jesus raising the dead. For example, when the messengers of John the Baptist ask Jesus if he is the Messiah, he responds, "the blind receive their sight, the lame walk, the lepers are cleansed, the deaf hear, *the dead are raised*, and the poor have good news brought to them" (Matt 11:5; also Luke 7:22). It is not only Jesus who raises the dead; it is his disciples as well. When he sends them on mission, he instructs them, "Cure the sick, *raise the dead*, cleanse the lepers, cast out demons" (Matt 10:8). To be sure, the dead whom Jesus raised during his earthly ministry died again since they were only restored to their former life. Their resurrection was not the beginning of the general resurrection from the dead whereby the dead enter into the transcendent realm of God's life through the power of the Spirit. Those whom Jesus and his disciples raised were restored to life but not yet changed and transformed by God's Spirit. These stories of Jesus raising the dead, however, play an important role in his proclamation of the inbreaking reign of God. For by raising the dead, Jesus and his disciples anticipate the general resurrection of the dead that will occur when the Son of Man returns in power and glory to inaugurate the final phase of God's kingdom. It is to these stories that I now turn.

The three Synoptic Gospels recount the story of Jesus raising Jairus's daughter. In doing so, they insert the account of the healing of a woman with a hemorrhage between the beginning and end of the story to increase the drama of the narrative. Jairus comes to Jesus, begging him to go and heal his *twelve*-year-old daughter, who is at the point of death (Mark 5:21-24). Jesus' departure, however, is delayed by a woman who has been afflicted with hemorrhages for *twelve* years (5:25-34). By the time he begins to go to Jairus's home it is too late. Jesus has lingered too long in attending to the older woman so that the young girl has died (5:35). Or at least it appears that she has died. In the final part of the story Jesus goes with Jairus, instructing him not to fear but to have faith (5:35-43). When Jesus enters Jairus's house, he insists that the child is not dead but only asleep. But those who are present are so sure that the girl is dead that they ridicule Jesus (5:40). In response to their ridicule, Jesus takes the child's father and mother, as well as his inner circle of Peter, James, and John, into the room where the child is. Grasping the child's hand, Jesus says, "Little girl, get up!" (literally, "I say to you arise," *soi legō egeire*; Mark 5:41).

Is the girl dead, as the mourners insist, or is she merely asleep, as Jesus says? Or, are both correct? From the point of view of the mourners the child is dead, because no matter what they do they cannot "wake" her. From the point of view of those without faith, those who do not accept Jesus' proclamation of the kingdom, the child has died. But Jesus looks at the child with the faith of one who knows that the power of God is already breaking into this world because the kingdom of God is making its appearance in his ministry. From the perspective of those who believe in the kingdom, then, the dead are merely asleep, waiting for the general resurrection from the dead. This mighty deed that Jesus performs, then, proclaims the inbreaking kingdom of God. It is not yet the beginning of the resurrection from the dead, and the child will die again. But what happens foreshadows what will happen in the final stage of the kingdom: the dead will rise incorruptible, never to die again. For those who fear and do not believe in the kingdom, the child was indeed dead, but for Jesus and those who believe in the kingdom, the child was asleep. In saying this, I do not mean that the child was sleeping and that Jesus found a clever way to awake her from her slumber. Rather, the dead child was asleep inasmuch as God's power is greater than the power of death.

There is another story in the Gospel of Mark that shares some interesting similarities with the story of Jairus's daughter. It occurs immediately after the transfiguration when another distraught father comes to Jesus for help (Mark 9:14-29). The father has already brought his demon-possessed son to Jesus' disciples, but the disciples have failed to expel the demon. Desperate, the man says to Jesus, "if you are able to do anything, have pity on us and help us," to which Jesus replies, "If you are able!—All things can be done for the one who believes," and the man replies, "I believe; help my unbelief!" (9:22-24). As in the episode of Jairus's daughter, the issue is faith. When Jesus finally expels the demon, Mark notes, "After crying out and convulsing him terribly, it came out, and the boy was like a corpse, *so that most of them said, 'He is dead'*" (9:26). As he did with Jairus's daughter, however, "Jesus took him by the hand and lifted him up, and he was able to stand" (9:27). Although this is an exorcism story, Mark wants us to remember what Jesus did for Jairus's daughter. Just as he took the little girl by the hand, so he lifts the young boy by the hand so that "he arose" (RSV). The story is not presented as a resurrection story, and it is only the crowd that thinks the boy is dead, but it would appear that Mark wants us to read this exorcism narrative as a resurrection story as well. For by lifting up the boy whom the demon has left as good as dead, Jesus has restored him to life. To be sure, the boy, like Jairus's daughter, will die again. What Jesus has done for both, however, points to the power of the inbreaking kingdom of God that will overcome death in a definitive way when Jesus returns as the glorious Son of Man.

The story of Jesus raising the widow's son, which is only found in the Gospel of Luke (7:11-17), is different from the accounts we have considered thus far as there is no doubt that the young man has died. Jesus, who has just healed the centurion's slave from a distance, now journeys to the city of Nain, where he encounters the funeral procession of a young man, the only son (*monogenēs*) of his widowed mother. Moved with pity for the woman, who has no one left to support her, Jesus tells her not to weep. And touching the coffin, he says to the dead youth, "Young man, I say to you, rise!" (7:14). While the verb that Jesus employs here (*egeirō*) can simply mean to stand up or rise, it is the same verb that the writers of the New Testament use when speaking of Jesus' resurrection. In raising the young man who is the only son of a widowed mother, then, Jesus foreshadows his own resurrection when the Father will raise his *only* Son.

The crowd that has been part of the funeral procession is filled with awe because it understands that it is standing in God's presence. Accordingly, the crowd glorifies God, just as the centurion will glorify God at Jesus' death (23:47) by exclaiming that a great prophet has arisen in its midst and that God has visited (*epeskepsato*) his people (7:16). This is the same word that Zechariah uses in his canticle when he speaks of God *visiting* and bringing redemption to his people (1:68) and the daybreak from on high *visiting* the people of Israel (1:78). Although the identification of Jesus as a great prophet is ultimately inadequate, it makes perfect sense here since the raising of the widow's son recalls the story of the great prophet Elijah, who raised the son of the widow of Zarephath (1 Kgs 17:17-24).

It is immediately after Jesus raises the widow's son, according to the Gospel of Luke, that the disciples of John the Baptist tell him all that Jesus has been doing. This leads John to send two of his disciples to ask if Jesus is the coming one or if they are to look for another. In response, Jesus instructs John's messengers to tell their master what they have seen and heard: "the blind receive their sight, the lame walk, the lepers are cleansed, the deaf hear, *the dead are raised*, the poor have good news brought to them" (7:22). The intent of Jesus' reply is evident. The mighty works he has been performing point to the dawn of the messianic age. By healing the sick, raising the dead, and preaching to the poor, Jesus inaugurates the messianic age. To be sure, the young man of Nain will die again since the general resurrection of the dead has not yet begun. His resurrection from the dead, however, signals what is about to happen with the death and resurrection of Israel's Messiah.

The account of the raising of Lazarus (which only appears in the Fourth Gospel) is the most explicit and theologically sophisticated account of Jesus raising someone from the dead. It is one of the seven signs that Jesus performs in the first half of the gospel, which is called the book of signs (John 1:19–12:50). The purpose of these signs is to point to Jesus as the one whom the Father has sent into the world to reveal the Father to the world so that the world may have life. As the seventh and last sign, the raising of Lazarus is the climax of the signs that Jesus performs, and its purpose is to point to him as the giver of life. Ironically, however, the very sign that points to Jesus as the giver of life is the sign that leads the Jewish leadership to plot Jesus' death (11:45-53).

The episode begins with Jesus learning that Lazarus is ill and affirming that this illness will not lead to death but to God's glory so that the Son may be gloried. As if to reinforce this, Jesus remains where he is for two days before going to Lazarus. When Jesus finally arrives at the home of Martha and Mary, Lazarus has already died and been in the tomb for four days. There is no doubt, then, that Lazarus is dead, and so also a great deal of puzzlement about Jesus' statement that this illness would not end in death. It is not surprising, then, that Martha complains even as she expresses her faith in Jesus: "Lord, if you had been here, my brother would not have died. But even now I know that God will give you whatever you ask of him" (11:21-22).

The conversation that ensues between Jesus and Martha is subtle and theologically charged. First, Jesus assures her that her brother will rise. Martha affirms this with an explicit statement of her faith in the general resurrection of the dead: "I know that he will rise again in the resurrection on the last day" (11:24). But Jesus has more in view than the general resurrection of the dead. He wants to lead Martha to a deeper understanding of resurrection life that is grounded in faith in him, a faith that overcomes the power of death even now. And so, he reveals, "*I am* the resurrection and the life. Those who believe in me, even though they die, will live, and everyone who lives and believes in me will never die. Do you believe this?" (11:25-26). Jesus is the resurrection and the life because he comes from the Father and does what the Father does: just as the Father raises the dead and gives them life, so Jesus raises the dead and gives them life (5:21). He calls himself the resurrection and the life because he raises the dead through the glory of the Father that has been bestowed upon him. When Jesus says that those who believe in him will live even if they die, he means that he will raise them on the last day. And when he says those who live and believe in him will never die, he means that even if they die they will not be separated from God because they already possess the seed of resurrection life through faith in him.

When Jesus comes to the tomb of Lazarus, he is deeply moved and troubled by the death of his friend, and he asks that the stone that covers the tomb be taken away. At this point, Martha reminds Jesus that Lazarus has been in the tomb for four days. *Lazarus is truly dead*, and there will be a great stench because the body is already decomposing. But Jesus reminds Martha that if she believes, she will see the glory of God. This glory of God is the glory the Father has bestowed on the Son, enabling the Son to raise the dead.

The story of the raising of Lazarus is the most theologically charged resurrection narrative we have encountered. Whereas the stories in the Synoptic Gospels hint at the general resurrection of the dead, the purpose of this account is to remind us that Jesus *is* the resurrection and the life. Those who believe in him are assured they will be raised from the dead, even if they die; and those who are raised from the dead will not die again. There will be no second death.

Lazarus, of course, died again. The resurrection he experienced was a return to his former existence rather than a transformation of his existence. His rising from the dead, however, is a sign that points to the fullness of resurrection life.

## Defending the Resurrection of the Dead

According to the Synoptic Gospels, there was an episode during the final days of Jesus' ministry in Jerusalem when he was challenged to defend the resurrection of the dead. This episode, which involves Jesus and the Sadducees, is one in a series of controversies between Jesus and the religious leaders in Jerusalem that occur shortly before his death. According to the Gospel of Mark, the Pharisees and some Herodians try to entrap Jesus by asking whether or not it is lawful for a Jew to pay taxes to the Roman emperor (12:13-17). Next, the Sadducees present Jesus with a case intended to show the difficulties inherent in the doctrine of the general resurrection of the dead (12:18-27). Finally, a scribe asks Jesus what the greatest commandment of the law is (12:28-34).

While the Pharisees and Sadducees may have been allied in their opposition to Jesus, they held opposing views about the resurrection of the dead, as Luke informs us in the Acts of the Apostles (Acts 23:8). Whereas the Pharisees embraced this rather new teaching on the resurrection of the dead, the Sadducees, who belonged to the priestly circles of the day, did not. Thus the purpose of their question is to demonstrate the problems inherent in the doctrine of the resurrection of the dead. This is why they present Jesus with the question they do. If the dead are raised, what will happen in the case of seven brothers, six of whom married the same woman at one point or another in order to raise up offspring for their deceased brother? If the dead are raised, as the Pharisees maintain, whose wife will she be after the resurrection of the dead since she was, at one time, married to each of the seven brothers? The fact that the Sadducees ask Jesus this strange question suggests that they know he espouses the teaching of the resurrection of the dead.

The response that Jesus gives, according to the gospels of Matthew and Mark, is essentially the same. First, he tells the Sadducees that they are wrong because they do not understand the Scriptures or the power of God. Second, they have misunderstood the nature of the resurrection from the dead. Resurrection from the dead is not a matter of resuscitation whereby people return to their former life, as the Sadducees seem to presuppose. It is entrance into a new kind of life in which there is no need to marry and propagate children since those who are raised do not die and so have no need to produce offspring; they will be like the angels in heaven who live forever. Scripture itself presupposes the resurrection of the dead, Jesus affirms. Quoting the passage from the book of Exodus in which God appears to Moses (Exod 3:6), he notes that God identifies himself as "the God of Abraham, the God of Isaac, and the God of Jacob" (Mark 12:26), which indicates that God has not abandoned the patriarchs who have died. Jesus concludes that the Sadducees are quite wrong because God is not the God of the dead but of the living (Mark 12:27). For even though Abraham, Isaac, and Jacob had been dead for centuries when God spoke to Moses, God still identifies himself as the God of Abraham, Isaac, and Jacob because they are alive in his sight.

Luke's version of this controversy is more expansive than the accounts of Mark and Matthew. In his response to the Sadducees, Jesus notes that whereas those who live in the present age marry, those who will be worthy to live in the age to come do not marry since they will be like the angels of God and will not die (Luke 20:34-36). Marriage is necessary in the present age to propagate the human race. But in the age to come, there will be no need to marry and propagate since the resurrected will not die.

The Sadducees, like the Corinthians whom Paul addresses in 1 Corinthians 15, have confused the resurrection with resuscitation from the dead. The more serious issue, however, is that they have underestimated the power of God. By denying the resurrection of the dead, they imply that the power of death is greater than the power of God, whereas the underlying claim of the resurrection from the dead is that God's power is stronger than death. To say that God is the God of the living rather than the God of the dead is to affirm that those who have died are alive before God because God has not abandoned them to death.

## Anticipating God's Vindication

The authors of the New Testament report that at different moments in his life, especially as he journeyed to Jerusalem, Jesus expressed his supreme confidence that his life and the central message of his ministry—the kingdom of God—would not end with his death. Rather he affirmed that God would vindicate him and the gospel he preached. Jesus expressed this faith in a series of statements that are often referred to as "passion predictions," a series of sayings in which he foretells his rejection, suffering, and death. These statements, however, are much more than "predictions" of Jesus' passion and death; they are statements in which he affirms that his suffering and death are an integral part of God's redemptive plan to usher in the kingdom of God. Accordingly, Jesus does not merely predict his suffering; he affirms his strong faith and hope that God will vindicate him by raising him from the dead, thereby ushering in a new phase of the kingdom of God.

If we follow the Gospel of Mark, the first of these statements occurs after Peter's confession at Caesarea Philippi that Jesus is the Messiah. Immediately after Peter's confession, Jesus tells the Twelve "that the Son of Man must undergo great suffering, and be rejected by the elders, the chief priests, and the scribes, and be killed, *and after three days rise again*" (8:31). Jesus' identification of himself as "the Son of Man" echoes Daniel 7, a passage in which Daniel has a vision of four beasts (each of which represents a nation that has oppressed Israel) arising from the sea. After these four beasts, a human figure, one like a son of man, comes with the clouds of heaven and is presented to God. "To him was given dominion / and glory and kingship, / that all peoples, nations, and languages / should serve him. / His dominion is an everlasting dominion / that shall not pass away, / and his kingship is one / that shall never be destroyed" (Dan 7:14). When Daniel asks who this figure is, he is told the following: "The kingship and dominion / and the greatness of the kingdoms under the whole heaven / shall be given to *the people of the holy ones of the Most High*; / their kingdom shall be an everlasting kingdom, / and all dominions shall serve and obey them" (Dan 7:27). The human figure in Daniel's vision, the one like a son of man, represents those loyal and faithful Israelites whom God will vindicate, after a period of suffering and persecution, by giving them an everlasting kingdom.

By referring to himself as "the Son of Man" Jesus appropriates this vision to interpret his destiny. His rejection and passion will not be in vain; they will be the prelude to his vindication. Just as the saints of the Most High received an everlasting kingdom after a period of persecution and suffering, so Jesus will be vindicated after his passion and death.

The most noticeable difference between the text of Daniel and Mark is the explicit reference to Jesus rising from the dead. The resurrection of the dead, however, is implicit in the text of Daniel 7 as the saints of the Most High have already died. Moreover, in Daniel 12:2-3 we find one of the earliest references to the resurrection of the dead: "Many of those who sleep in the dust of the earth shall awake, some to everlasting life, and some to shame and everlasting contempt. Those who are wise shall shine like the brightness of the sky, and those who lead many to righteousness, like the stars forever and ever." Jesus' affirmation of his resurrection from the dead, therefore, is firmly grounded in the hope of vindication and resurrection found in the book of Daniel. He understands that he must be rejected, suffer, and die in order to usher in the kingdom of God he has proclaimed throughout his ministry. He is confident that God will vindicate him at the resurrection of the dead by granting him life in the kingdom of God. The kingdom of God and the resurrection of the dead are intimately related to each other inasmuch as resurrection from the dead is entrance into the fullness of God's kingdom.

Jesus affirms that God will vindicate him a second and a third time as he makes his way to Jerusalem, where he knows he must suffer and die. The second statement of vindication is the shortest of the three, but it makes the same point—Jesus will rise from the dead: "The Son of Man is to be betrayed into human hands, and they will kill him, *and three days after being killed, he will rise again*" (Mark 9:31). The third is the most detailed, outlining the events that will take place during Jesus' passion, but it concludes in the same way, with a hope for future vindication: "See, we are going up to Jerusalem, and the Son of Man will be handed over to the chief priests and the scribes, and they will condemn him to death; then they will hand him over to the Gentiles; they will mock him, and spit upon him, and flog him, and kill him; *and after three days he will rise again*" (10:33-34).

Two points should be noted here. First, Jesus' disciples do not comprehend the significance of these statements in which he affirms that he will rise after three days. Indeed, after the transfiguration, when Jesus tells Peter, James, and John not to recount what they have seen until after the Son of Man has risen from the dead, Mark notes the following: "So they kept the matter to themselves, *questioning what this rising from the dead could mean*" (9:10). Second, whereas the New Testament usually speaks of *God raising Jesus from the dead*, in these statements Jesus speaks of *the Son of Man rising from the dead after three days.*

In regard to the first point, the fact that Jesus' disciples are puzzled by his statements of rising from the dead is not surprising. Indeed, it is to be expected since the Pharisaic doctrine of the resurrection from the dead was a relatively new teaching that was not accepted by all, as the controversy between Jesus and the Sadducees shows. While the disciples witnessed Jesus raising people from the dead, they did not understand that God would raise the dead in a final and definitive way, at the end of the ages. Second, in saying that he would rise from the dead, Jesus is affirming his hope in the resurrection of the death rather than claiming that he will raise himself by his own power. When he says that the Son of Man will rise after three days, he is affirming his faith and trust that God will vindicate him shortly after his death. Luke, who makes use of the Gospel of Mark in writing his gospel, clarifies this when he edits Mark in this way: "The Son of Man must undergo great suffering, and be rejected by the elders, chief priests, and scribes, and be killed, *and on the third day be raised*" (Luke 9:22). The fact that Luke maintains Mark's language about rising from the dead in Jesus' third statement of vindication (Luke 18:33) does not contradict what I have just said but rather indicates that Luke understands "rising from the dead" in terms of "God raising Jesus from the dead." Thus, while Luke uses both expressions (rising from the dead, and being raised from the dead), he understands rising from the dead in light of being raised from the dead.

In addition to these statements of suffering and vindication, there are others in which Jesus anticipates that God will vindicate him after his death. For example, he speaks of his return at the end of the ages as the glorious and triumphant Son of Man (Mark 8:38; 13:26-27; 14:62; also see Luke 17:22-37). He says that the next Passover he will celebrate with his disciples will be in the kingdom of God (Mark 14:25), and he tells his disciples that after he has been raised up he will go ahead of them to Galilee, where they will see him (Mark 14:28; see 16:7 as well). Furthermore, according to the Gospel of Matthew, the priests and Pharisees ask Pilate to secure Jesus' tomb with a guard, for they remember "what that impostor said while he was still alive, 'After three days I will rise again'" (Matt 27:63). The upshot of this is as follows: *Jesus' faith that God would vindicate him by raising him from the dead undergirds and complements his central teaching about the kingdom of God since the kingdom will be experienced in its fullness at the resurrection of the dead.* There is no tension, then, between Jesus' proclamation of the kingdom of God and the church's kerygma that the resurrection of the dead is at hand—for the Messiah has been raised from the dead, the firstfruits of the general resurrection of the dead.

## The Kingdom of God and the Resurrection from the Dead

Before concluding this chapter, I would like to reflect further on the relationship between Jesus' proclamation of the kingdom of God and his resurrection from the dead. By all accounts, the central content of Jesus' proclamation was that the kingdom of God was making its appearance in his ministry. It was in light of the inbreaking rule of God that Jesus called people to repent and gathered a community of disciples in order to renew Israel. Jesus' ministry, however, did not conclude with the final inbreaking of the kingdom, and after his death the central message of the early church tended to focus on his saving death and life-giving resurrection. Thus *the one who*

*proclaimed the gospel of the kingdom became the content of the gospel
the early church proclaimed.* This is not to say that the early church
forgot or neglected Jesus' proclamation of the kingdom of God; it did
not. But it does raise the question of the relationship between Jesus'
proclamation of the kingdom of God and the church's proclamation
of Jesus' death and resurrection. How are the two related? How is
it that the one who proclaimed the gospel of the kingdom became
the content of the church's gospel?

Although Jesus proclaimed that the kingdom of God was making its appearance in his ministry, he was careful to teach his disciples "the mystery" of the kingdom of God—namely, that while the
kingdom is *already* present in his ministry, the kingdom will not be
revealed in power and glory until the glorious Son of Man returns at
the end of the ages to gather the elect. "Son of Man" is Jesus' chosen
self-designation that allows him to speak of himself in a way that is
both self-effacing and revealing. On the one hand, a listener might
think that Jesus is merely referring to his humanity. But the biblically
literate reader, who is familiar with Daniel 7, knows that "the one like
a son of man" in the book of Daniel was a figure who, after a period
of persecution and suffering, received kingship, power, and glory
from God. When Jesus refers to himself as the Son of Man, then, he
employs a term that is both elusive and revealing. While it can refer
to his humanity, it also refers to his destiny as the messianic Son of
God. Jesus is God's chosen agent whom God will vindicate after a
period of suffering and rejection. Accordingly, when he teaches his
disciples that he will return as the glorious Son of Man to usher in
the final stage of the kingdom of God, he is saying that *the resurrection is intimately related to the establishment of the kingdom of God
since Jesus cannot return as the glorious Son of Man to inaugurate the
kingdom until he has been raised from the dead.*

The relationship between Jesus' proclamation of the kingdom of
God and his resurrection from the dead can be put in this way. By
his ministry of preaching, healing, and teaching, Jesus inaugurated
the kingdom of God. In his person, the kingdom of God was made
present to those who believed in his message of the kingdom. Those
who did not believe in his message and those who were looking

for a restoration of the kingdom of David eventually saw Jesus as a failure, a false prophet. The final stage of the kingdom of God that Jesus proclaimed could only be brought about by an act of God raising Jesus from the dead. *By his resurrection from the dead, Jesus was the first to enter into the fullness of the kingdom.* Understood in this way, the kingdom of God and the resurrection are so intimately related to each other that to proclaim one is to proclaim the other. Those who are raised from the dead have entered into the fullness of the kingdom, and those who have entered into the fullness of the kingdom have been raised from the dead.

If what I have said is correct, there is no tension between the proclamation of Jesus and the church's proclamation of his death and resurrection. Both proclaim the same message. Jesus proclaims that the kingdom of God is making its appearance in his ministry, and the church proclaims that Jesus has been raised from the dead, the first to enter into the fullness of the kingdom. By proclaiming the death and resurrection of its Lord, the church confesses that her Lord has entered into the fullness of the kingdom, thereby making it possible for all who believe in him to do the same.

Chapter 2

# The Witness of
# the Resurrection Narratives

In the previous chapter I examined material in the gospels that pertained to Jesus' resurrection and the resurrection of the dead apart from the resurrection narratives proper. In this chapter I consider the gospel narratives that deal with Jesus' resurrection. Before proceeding to this task, however, it is necessary to state what I will and will not do.

*I will not discuss the historicity of the resurrection and the events surrounding it.* Put another way, I am not trying to prove that the resurrection happened. Others have undertaken this apologetic task, and so I begin with the following premise of faith: *God raised Jesus from the dead.* My purpose, then, is not to defend this statement but to explain what it means for those who believe in Jesus' resurrection from the dead.[1]

*I will not reconstruct how the resurrection narratives came about.* Others have undertaken this complicated task, and I make use of their work.[2] Rather, I begin with the gospel narratives as we have them in order to explain what they proclaim about the resurrection.[3] Accordingly, I will interpret the train of thought in each of the gospel narratives. By doing this, I hope to clarify what each gospel contributes to our understanding of Jesus' resurrection, which is the foundation of our hope in the resurrection of the dead.

*My interpretation of the resurrection narratives is an exercise in biblical theology rather than historical reconstruction.* This statement assumes that the resurrection narratives can be approached in different ways: in terms of their historical reliability or in terms of their theological meaning. When they are studied in terms of history, the primary question of the interpreter is, what happened? For example, was the tomb empty? Who was present at the tomb? To whom did Jesus appear? Did people truly see the risen Lord, or did they merely have a religious experience that he was risen and alive?

My study of the resurrection narratives looks at the material from a different vantage point. Instead of asking what happened, I seek to understand *the theological significance of what happened.* What does it mean to say that God raised Jesus from the dead? What is the implication of this statement for those who believe that God raised Jesus from the dead? In addressing these questions, I begin with the following faith premises: (1) God raised Jesus from the dead, (2) the tomb was empty, (3) and the risen Lord appeared to chosen witnesses. In other words, I begin with the premise that God vindicated Jesus' preaching about the kingdom of God by raising him to a new kind of life—resurrection life—whereby Jesus entered into the fullness of the kingdom of God that he preached because he entered into the fullness of God's life.

*I will not harmonize the resurrection narratives of Matthew, Mark, Luke, and John.* As we move through these narratives, it will become apparent that there are significant differences in the way each evangelist relates the narrative of Jesus' resurrection. For example, in the gospels of Matthew and Mark the disciples are told to go to Galilee in order to see the risen Lord, but in the Gospel of Luke the resurrection appearances occur in and around Jerusalem. While differences such as these may be disturbing to some, I hope to show that they are attempts on the part of the first Christians to make sense of the "mystery" of the resurrection.

*I approach the resurrection of Jesus as an event rooted in history but transcending history.* On the one hand, the resurrection is rooted in history inasmuch as Jesus of Nazareth lived at a particular time and place. On the other hand, the resurrection of Jesus is a transcendent event that cannot be fully comprehended because the risen Jesus entered into an entirely new realm of existence that we have yet to experience. Put another way, the resurrection does not mean that Jesus was restored to his former way of life. For, if that is all that happened to him, then Jesus would have had to die again, as did Lazarus and the son of the widow at Nain. To confess that God raised Jesus from the dead is to confess that God raised him into the sphere of his own life, a life we cannot comprehend until we have experienced it. This is why the New Testament writers never describe the event of Jesus' resurrection from the dead.[4] Instead, they recount the story of the empty tomb and the appearances of the risen one to his chosen witnesses, but they never portray Jesus being raised from the dead. Although countless artists have portrayed Jesus' resurrection from the dead, the gospel writers seem to have understood that God's powerful deed in raising Jesus from the dead is a transcendent event that goes beyond human description.[5] Accordingly, although they affirm that God raised Jesus from the dead, they do not describe how this occurred.

In the remainder of this chapter I deal with the gospel narratives of Jesus' resurrection in the following order: Mark, Matthew, Luke, and John. I begin with the Gospel of Mark because most scholars argue (correctly, in my view) that Mark is the earliest of the four gospels to have been written and that Matthew and Luke made use of it in the composition of their gospels. I conclude with the Gospel of John because it seems to have been written after the composition of the other three gospels, and while its author may have known one or more of the other gospels, he does not use these gospels in the way that Matthew and Luke use the Gospel of Mark as a source.

## The Resurrection Narrative in the Gospel according to Mark

The Gospel of Mark presents a special challenge to interpreters since the canonical form of the gospel we have inherited has multiple endings. The oldest of these endings is the story of the empty tomb (Mark 16:1-8). But in addition to this ending, there is a shorter ending and a longer ending of the Gospel of Mark that provides the gospel with a sense of closure not found in the oldest ending of the gospel.[6]

The oldest ending of the gospel (16:1-8) presents a further problem because of the enigmatic way in which it concludes: with the women fleeing from the tomb in fear without saying anything to anyone about what they experienced. Was this the original ending of the gospel? If so, why did Mark end his gospel with the women saying nothing of what they had seen and without the risen Lord appearing to anyone? Or, was there a more satisfying ending that was lost? The presence of the shorter and longer endings, which bring a sense of closure to the gospel, indicate that the earliest readers of the gospel felt a need for a more satisfying conclusion to this elusive gospel. Since it is impossible to prove or disprove that the original ending of the gospel was lost or mutilated, I will try to make sense of this original ending in light of the entire gospel story before considering the longer ending of the gospel, which the Roman Catholic Church considers to be part of its canonical Scripture, even if these endings did not come from the hand of the evangelist.

### The Empty Tomb

The story of the empty tomb unfolds in the following way: The women make preparations to anoint the body of Jesus and go to the tomb (16:1-2). The women discover that the stone has been rolled away (16:3-4). The women enter the tomb and encounter a young man (16:5). The young man explains why the tomb is empty and instructs the women to tell Jesus' disciples and Peter to go to Galilee (16:6-7). The women leave in fear without saying anything to anyone (16:8).

The story of the empty tomb is closely related to the account of Jesus' death in Mark 15. Jesus died on Friday and the women who witnessed his death (15:40) and burial (15:47) returned home and observed the Sabbath. When the Sabbath was over, the women (Mary of Magdalene, Mary the mother of James, and Salome) return to the tomb with the intention of anointing Jesus (16:1). While their intention is admirable, the reader of the gospel knows that Jesus had already been anointed for burial before his death when an unnamed woman anointed his head with a costly ointment (14:3-9). Thus the attentive reader understands there is no need for the women to anoint Jesus, for his body has already been anointed for burial (14:8).

As they come to anoint Jesus, the women ask who will roll the stone from the tomb for them (16:1), a difficulty one would have expected them to have anticipated before setting out on their mission. Their concern, however, is ill-founded, for when they arrive the rock "had already been rolled back" (16:4). The use of the passive voice here, what grammarians refer to as "the divine passive," points to the intervention of God. Joseph of Arimathea had rolled the large stone against the door of the tomb (15:46), presumably to safeguard the body, but the stone *has been rolled back* by the power of God.

When the women enter the tomb, they meet a young man dressed in white, sitting on the right side of the tomb. Although Mark does not identify the young man as an angel, the message he bears indicates that he is a heavenly messenger who has come to announce the meaning of the empty tomb to the women. The women are looking for Jesus of Nazareth who had been crucified, but he is no longer there because *"he has been raised"* (16:6). Once more the passive voice points to God's action: The power of God removed the stone from the door of the tomb, and the power of God has raised Jesus from the dead. Having clarified the meaning of the empty tomb, the young man instructs the women to tell Jesus' disciples and Peter that "he is going ahead of you to Galilee; there you will see him, just as he told you" (16:7). The young man's message is an unmistakable echo of Jesus' words to Peter and the disciples at the Last Supper: "You will all become deserters; for it is written, / 'I will strike the shepherd, / and the sheep will be scattered.' / But after I am raised up, I will go before you to Galilee" (14:27-28). For those who heard the interpretative words of the young man at the tomb, there is no doubt about what has happened: Jesus has been raised from the dead by God.

The most puzzling part of the story is the last verse. The women, who have heard this interpretation of the empty tomb, flee in fear "and they said nothing to anyone, for they were afraid" (16:8). That they flee in fear is not surprising since they have been in the presence of a heavenly being. The young man whom they have encountered is not a human being; he is God's messenger; he is an angel. What is surprising is that the women say nothing to anyone, for they were afraid. How are we to interpret this abrupt ending? Here there are two lines of interpretation.

First, some scholars argue that the women told the disciples and Peter what the young man told them, even though this is not narrated in the text. According to this interpretation, the women said nothing to anyone on the way but went immediately to the disciples because they were filled with awe and fear at what they experienced.[7] Scholars who support this line of argument, with which I agree, note that at the Last Supper Jesus tells his disciples, "But after I am raised up, I will go before you to Galilee" (14:28). Thus, even though the evangelist never narrates the meeting between Jesus and his disciples, he assures his readers that this meeting will take place, thereby suggesting that the women did fulfill their mission: they did not speak to anyone on the way, but they did communicate the young man's message to the disciples.

Second, other scholars maintain that the silence of the women was absolute; they did not communicate the message of the young man to the disciples. Here there are two approaches. Those who adopt a purely historical perspective argue that there was never a meeting between Jesus and his disciples according to the Markan gospel with the result that the disciples were not legitimate witnesses to the resurrection. Those who adopt a literary approach do not deny that the risen Lord appeared to the disciples, but they do argue that Mark portrays the women as failing in their mission in order to show that God is victorious even though all of the human characters in the story eventually fail,[8] or to invite the reader to do what the women do not do: to announce the resurrection.[9] While I am in sympathy with these literary approaches inasmuch as they provide a reason for the silence that requires readers to rethink their assumptions about how God acts and to become involved in the work of evangelization, I am inclined to give greater emphasis to Jesus' promise at the Last Supper that he will meet his disciples in Galilee (14:28). In my view, Mark wants us to understand that the women fulfilled their mission even though he does not narrate how they did so. And by his ending, he invites us to go to Galilee, that is, to follow Jesus in the way of discipleship and proclaim the good news of the resurrection.

### A Shorter Ending

Given the enigmatic way in which the Gospel of Mark ends (according to the best manuscripts available to us), it is not surprising that other endings of the gospel developed. While we do not know how these endings came about or who wrote them, we can assume that they were produced by scribes who sought to give the gospel a more satisfying sense of closure than is found in Mark 16:1-8.

One such ending is "the shorter ending of Mark," which does not have a verse number assigned to it. While this ending usually occurs with the longer ending of Mark (16:9-20), it is also found independently of the longer ending in a few manuscripts. This shorter ending reads as follows:

> And all that had been commanded them they told briefly to those around Peter. And afterward Jesus himself sent out through them, from east to west, the sacred and imperishable proclamation of eternal salvation.

This ending brings closure to the gospel in two ways. First, it explicitly says that the women did what the young man at the tomb instructed them to do: they told Peter and the disciples that the risen Lord has gone to Galilee, where they will see him as he told them. Second, this ending notes that the gospel was preached by the disciples whom the Lord sent out with the message—the kerygma—of eternal life. The ending, however, does not recount the promised meeting between Jesus and the disciples in Galilee, nor does it report any appearances of the risen Lord to them. Thus, while the ending is satisfying insofar as it brings closure to the gospel in a way that Mark 16:1-8 does not, it remains unsatisfying inasmuch as it does not narrate an appearance of the risen Lord to his disciples.

### A Longer Ending

In addition to the shorter ending, the manuscript tradition witnesses to a longer ending that narrates multiple appearances of the risen Lord. Although this ending was produced by someone other than the evangelist, whoever composed it was keenly aware of a major Markan theme: the persistent failure of the disciples to believe. The ending consists of four units: an appearance of the risen Lord to Mary Magdalene (16:9-11), an appearance to two disciples (16:12-13), an appearance to all the disciples whom the risen Lord commissions to preach the gospel (16:14-18), and the Lord's ascension (16:19-20).

In the first unit, the risen Christ appears to Mary Magdalene, the one who witnessed the Lord's death (15:40) and burial (15:47), and came to the tomb to anoint his body (16:1). This appearance is unrelated to the ending in Mark 16:1-8 considering that there is no mention of the empty tomb or the other women. Having risen from the dead, Jesus appears to Mary on Easter morning, and Mary immediately tells Jesus' followers, who are still weeping and worrying, of the appearance. But they do not believe her.

In the second unit, the risen Lord appears "in another form" to two disciples who are walking in the country. Exactly what this means is not explained, but it does indicate that Jesus' resurrection was not a mere resuscitation, a return to his former bodily life. When they return to tell the other disciples of the appearance, the other disciples refuse to believe them just as they refused to believe Mary.

In the third unit, the risen Lord appears to the eleven disciples as they are sitting at a table, thereby suggesting a eucharistic motif. The Lord's message is twofold. First, he reprimands them for their lack of faith. Second, he commissions them to proclaim the gospel to all, declaring that those who believe and are baptized will be saved, whereas those who do not believe will be condemned, and promising that strong signs will accompany their preaching.

The longer ending concludes with a brief account of the Lord's ascension and a description of the disciples proclaiming the gospel, which the Lord confirmed by many signs.

The longer ending is the most satisfying of the three endings. It brings closure to the gospel story by narrating a number of appearances of the risen Lord, as well as an account of his ascension. Moreover, its author skillfully makes use of a prominent theme of the gospel: the incomprehension of the disciples who refuse to believe in the Lord's resurrection, even when eyewitnesses attest that he is risen and alive. The longer ending, like the shorter one, however, does not recount a meeting of the disciples in Galilee. Like the Lukan gospel, it seems to presuppose that the risen Christ appeared to his disciples in Jerusalem (although this is never explicitly stated).

## *The Meaning of the Markan Resurrection Narratives*

Since the Gospel of Mark has three different endings, it will be best to consider the theological meaning of each ending separately, beginning with the oldest (16:1-8).

There are two dimensions to the way in which Mark 16:1-8 ends the gospel. First, the gospel ends with the story of the empty tomb without recording any appearances of the risen Lord to his apostles. Second, because the gospel ends without recounting the appearance of the risen Christ to his disciples in Galilee, the gospel concludes without a sense of closure. By concluding in such an open-ended manner, without recording any appearances of the risen Lord, the gospel challenges readers to confront the fact of the empty tomb. What is the meaning and significance of this event? Has the body been removed by someone, or has Jesus of Nazareth, the one who was crucified, been raised from the dead? The messenger at the tomb, of course, provides readers with the proper answer: he is not here because God has raised him from the dead. But the message itself—even though it comes from a heavenly messenger—does not exempt readers of the gospel from making their own act of faith.

At the end of this gospel, it is left to readers to accept or reject the message of the young man. Those who accept the message understand that the empty tomb is God's response to the death of his Son. The Son, who experienced the full anguish of death to the point of crying out, "My God, my God, why have you forsaken me?" (15:34), has been vindicated by God because, trusting in the power of God to save him, he refused to save himself (15:29-32). The rock that has been rolled away is a sign for those who believe in the powerful way in which God has intervened to save his Son. Whereas human beings sought to confine the Son in the tomb, God has broken the power of death that appeared to have defeated the Son of God and called into question his proclamation of the kingdom of God. With Jesus' resurrection the kingdom of God enters a new stage as the Son of God enters into the kingdom he proclaimed.

The shorter ending of Mark's gospel provides the closure that is lacking in the oldest ending, but it does not have the theological depth of the older ending. It is not, however, without theological significance. By recounting how the risen Lord sends his disciples "from east to west" this ending testifies to the universal significance of "the sacred and imperishable" message that the disciples preached. What happened on the cross and what God did in raising Jesus from the dead has significance for the salvation of the world.

The longer ending, which recounts a number of appearances of the risen Lord, makes two theological points. First, the disciples failed to believe the message of their Lord's resurrection when Mary Magdalene and two other disciples announced it to them. The resurrection of Jesus, then, does not do away with the need for faith; it requires faith. Second, even though the disciples failed to believe the message that was spoken to them, the risen Lord does not reject them. The risen Lord will not allow his disciples' lack of faith to frustrate God's plan of salvation. After reprimanding them for their lack of faith, he commissions them to preach to the entire creation the gospel of his death and resurrection, which they failed to understand. Human beings will always fail, but their failure cannot frustrate God's plan.

Finally, none of these endings attempt to portray the resurrection or the risen Lord. What happened at the resurrection is a transcendent event that cannot be described. By raising Jesus from the dead, God shared his own life with the crucified Jesus of Nazareth, a life that cannot be described because it is beyond the realm of what we know. There is, however, continuity since the risen one is the crucified one.

## The Resurrection Narrative in the Gospel according to Matthew

The most satisfying ending of the Gospel of Mark is the ending that concludes the Gospel of Matthew! In addition to assuring us that the women announced the angel's message to the disciples, it relates the promised meeting in Galilee between the risen Lord and his disciples. Moreover, it contains a theme that occurs throughout the Gospel of Mark: the failure of the disciples to believe. For, even when the disciples see the risen Lord in Galilee, some of them doubt (28:17). While it is possible that Matthew was aware of a lost ending of the Gospel of Mark, most scholars believe it is more likely he edited and expanded the ending of Mark 16:1-8. Whatever the case, I proceed on the assumption that Matthew knew the Gospel of Mark, editing and expanding it in light of traditions available to him and his own understanding of the resurrection.

The main events of the Matthean resurrection narrative are as follows. First, the chief priests and the Pharisees ask Pilate to post a guard at the tomb lest Jesus' disciples steal the body (27:62-66). Second, as Mary Magdalene and another Mary arrive at the tomb, the angel rolls back the stone and announces the resurrection. As the women leave the tomb, the risen Lord appears to them (28:1-10). Third, the guards tell the chief priests what has happened and the priests bribe them to say that the disciples stole the body (28:11-15). Fourth, the disciples meet the risen Lord in Galilee, and he commissions them to preach the gospel to all the nations (28:16-20). The most distinctive element of the Matthean account is the addition of the two episodes about the guards. These episodes introduce a strong apologetic motif into the Matthean resurrection narrative that counters the claim that the tomb was empty because Jesus' disciples had stolen his body.

### *The Guard at the Tomb*

Matthew prefaces his resurrection narrative with a story that is only found in his gospel: the posting of a guard at the tomb. Echoing the statements that Jesus made about his passion and resurrection earlier in the gospel, the chief priests and Pharisees inform Pilate how Jesus said that he would rise after three days (16:21; 17:23; 20:19). Fearful that Jesus' disciples will steal his body and then proclaim that he has risen from the dead, they ask Pilate to secure the tomb until the third day. In response, Pilate tells them to take a guard and make the tomb "as secure as you can" (27:65). The perceptive reader, however, knows that no matter how secure the religious leaders make the tomb, they will not be able to secure it from the power of God.

### The Empty Tomb

While it is apparent that Matthew knew the story of the empty tomb as found in the Markan gospel, it is clear that he has edited Mark's account in order to highlight the power of the resurrection and assure readers that the women communicated the message of the angel to the disciples. The account begins with Mary Magdalene and another Mary (there is no mention of Salome) coming to the tomb, not to anoint the body of Jesus but to see the tomb, which they last saw on the day of Jesus' death when a great stone was rolled across its entrance (27:60-61). Since the women go to see the tomb rather than to anoint the body, there is no discussion about who will roll the stone away for them, as there is in Mark's account.

When they come to the tomb, there is a great earthquake as the angel of the Lord descends from heaven to remove the stone. This earthquake is reminiscent of the earthquake that occurred after Jesus' death when the tombs of many were opened and the bodies of Israel's holy ones were raised and then, after Jesus' own resurrection, appeared to many in Jerusalem (27:51-53). Just as that earthquake highlighted the transcendent power of God that inaugurated the beginning of the new age through the death of his Son, so this earthquake highlights the transcendent power of God that raised Jesus from the dead. While the removal of the stone would have been the perfect time for Matthew to describe Jesus coming out of the tomb, there is no description of the resurrection because the resurrection is a transcendent event that defies description. The removal of the stone is a sign of the resurrection, not its cause.

While the angel tells the women not to fear, the guards who were guarding the *dead* Jesus become as *dead* men from fear of what has happened. The angel then instructs the women to tell Jesus' disciples that *he has been raised from the dead* just as he told them (16:21; 17:23; 20:19) and is going before them to Galilee (28:7; see 26:32). In obedience to the angel's message, the women leave in order to relate the angel's message to Jesus' disciples (28:8). But as they do, the risen Lord appears to them (making them the first witnesses to the resurrection), and they worship him. Repeating the angel's message, the risen Christ instructs the women to tell his "brothers," the disciples, that they will see him in Galilee (28:10).

## The Guards and the Religious Leaders

Following these events, Matthew relates the reaction of the guards whom the chief priests and Pharisees asked Pilate to post lest the disciples steal Jesus' body and say he has been raised from the dead (27:64). Pilate's reply ("make it as secure as you can," 27:65) is ironic. The religious leaders will secure the tomb as best they can, but their doing so will not prevent God from reversing their judgment against his Son by breaking open the tomb and overcoming the power of death.

When the guards report what has happened, the chief priests refuse to believe that Jesus *has been raised* from the dead—even though they have been told of the earthquake occasioned by the descent of the angel of the Lord. Instead, just as they gave Judas thirty pieces of silver to betray Jesus (26:15), so they bribe the guards to say that Jesus' disciples stole his body while they were asleep. For Matthew, this episode explains the origin of the rumor that Jesus' disciples stole his body from the tomb, a rumor that was already circulating when Matthew was writing (28:15).

## The Disciples and the Risen Lord

Having explained how the rumor about the disciples stealing the body of Jesus originated, Matthew concludes with the promised meeting of Jesus and his disciples in Galilee. In obedience to the women's report, the disciples go to the mountain in Galilee that Jesus had designated for the meeting in Galilee, and there they see him. Like the magi who worshiped the child Jesus (2:11) and like the women who worshiped the risen Lord (28:9), they worship the risen Christ (28:17). Despite seeing and worshiping him, however, some doubt, thereby indicating a continuing lack of faith and suggesting that the appearance of the risen Christ does not relieve one of the need to believe in the resurrection.

Rather than reprimand his disciples, the risen Lord assures them that God has granted him all authority in heaven and on earth. Earlier the religious leaders asked Jesus by what authority he acted (21:28); now there can be no doubt that his authority comes from God.

On the basis of this authority, Jesus commissions his disciples to preach the gospel to all nations. Whereas previously he had only sent them on mission to "the lost sheep of the house of Israel" (10:6), now he instructs them to "make disciples of all nations" (28:19), baptizing in the name of the Father, the Son, and the Holy Spirit. This trinitarian formula highlights the exalted status of the risen Christ who now belongs to the same realm as God and the Spirit. Jesus, of course, was always the Son of God (3:17; 14:33; 16:16; 27:54). At his resurrection, however, he attains a new status: he is now the exalted and risen Son of God whose authority can no longer be questioned.

In addition to baptizing people in the name of the Father, the Son, and the Holy Spirit, the disciples are to teach them all that Jesus taught them. Teaching was a central element of Jesus' ministry. On numerous occasions, Matthew summarizes Jesus' ministry in terms of teaching, preaching, and healing (4:23; 9:35; 11:1). And on five occasions, Jesus delivers discourses, the most memorable being his great Sermon on the Mount (5–7). Jesus' disciples are now to do what he did: they are to make disciples just as he made disciples by teaching others as he taught them.

Matthew concludes his gospel with the risen Lord's promise to be with them until the end of the ages. This promise echoes the explanation of Jesus' name "Emmanuel" (1:23), and Jesus' promise to be with his church whenever two or three gather in his name (18:20). Because he has been raised from the dead, Jesus can fulfill this promise. No longer confined to the dimensions of time and space, the risen Lord will be with the church throughout the ages.

## The Meaning of the Matthean Resurrection Narrative

In addition to providing readers with a satisfying ending, the resurrection narrative of Matthew offers them further theological insight into the meaning of Jesus' resurrection.

First, the manner in which Matthew composed his account of the empty tomb highlights the transcendent power of God that was at work in raising Jesus from the dead. The descent of the angel who rolls away the stone causes a great earthquake. This earthquake, which recalls the great earthquake that opened the tombs of many at the moment of Jesus' death, indicates that the new age of the resurrection of the dead has begun in the resurrection of God's Son. This dramatic explanation of how the stone was removed points to the power of God who frustrates the efforts of human beings to confine the body of the crucified Jesus to the tomb. Thus, the resurrection of Jesus marks the beginning of a new age, the resurrection of the dead, which was foreshadowed by the resurrection of many holy people in Jerusalem at Jesus' death (27:52).

Second, the refusal of the soldiers and religious leaders to believe in the resurrection of Jesus in the face of this apocalyptic event underlines the hardness of the human heart that can resist the most powerful evidence. The resurrection is God's response to his Son's death; it is God's judgment on those who put his Son to death. But not even the resurrection can change the hearts of those who refuse to be changed. The resurrection must be received and appropriated by faith.

Third, the resurrection leads to evangelization, to preaching the gospel to the nations. It is not enough to believe in the resurrection; one must proclaim the resurrection to others. This is why Jesus' commission to his disciples is so important. Whereas the purpose of his ministry was to preach to the lost sheep of Israel in order to renew and restore Israel (15:24), the purpose of his disciples' ministry is to preach the gospel to all nations (28:19). The resurrection, which is the climax and ending of the story of Jesus' ministry, is the starting point and beginning of his disciples' ministry in every generation until he comes again.

Finally, the reaction of some of the disciples at the mountain in Galilee indicates that the resurrection is not a substitute for faith but the origin and basis of faith. Even those who see the Lord must believe. Those who have not seen the risen Christ are not at a disadvantage since even those who have seen the Lord must believe in the resurrection.

# The Resurrection Narrative in the Gospel according to Luke

The Gospel of Luke, like the Gospel of Matthew, provides its readers with a more satisfying ending to the gospel than does the earliest ending of Mark's gospel (Mark 16:1-8). The women tell the disciples what they have discovered at the tomb, and Jesus appears to his disciples, who continue to find it difficult to believe. Unlike the ending of the Gospel of Matthew, however, the ending of Luke's gospel is not an appropriate ending for the Gospel of Mark. For even though the women report what they have encountered at the tomb, there is no mention of Jesus going ahead of his disciples to Galilee, where they will meet him. In the Gospel of Luke all of the appearances of the risen Lord occur in or near Jerusalem. Thus, even though Luke may have known the ending of Mark's gospel, his gospel reflects a tradition about the resurrection that focuses on Jerusalem rather than on Galilee. Given the central role Jerusalem plays in Luke's gospel, this is not surprising.[10]

Luke 24 manifests a clearly defined structure that can be summarized in this way. The women go to the tomb, where they encounter two men dressed in radiant garments who tell them that Jesus has been raised from the dead. Despite the women's report, the apostles do not believe (24:1-12). Next, the risen Lord appears to two disciples who are leaving Jerusalem to go to Emmaus. But they do not recognize the stranger on the way as the risen Lord until he explains the Scriptures to them and breaks bread with them. When the two report to the eleven apostles what has happened, the apostles are already discussing the resurrection because the Lord has appeared to Simon/Peter (24:13-35). The risen Lord then appears to all of the apostles. After explaining the Scriptures to them, he commissions them to preach in his name to all the nations, beginning from Jerusalem (24:36-49).

Finally, after the risen one is taken up into heaven, the eleven apostles return to Jerusalem, where they praise God in the temple (24:50-53). The motif that unifies this carefully structured chapter is the need for the Messiah to suffer and die before entering his glory.

### *The Empty Tomb*

As in the Gospel of Mark, the women come to the tomb after the Sabbath with the intent of anointing Jesus' body, a detail that makes more sense in the Lukan gospel since there is no account of a woman anointing Jesus' body for burial in the Lukan passion narrative.[11] When the women arrive at the tomb, they find that the stone has been rolled away, and upon entering the tomb they do not find Jesus' body. Instead, they encounter two men dressed in dazzling garments who ask why they are seeking the living among the dead. The men, who will be identified as angels, remind the women of what Jesus told them while he was still with them: that the Son of Man must be handed over to sinners who will crucify him, but that he will rise on the third day (see Luke 9:44). This admonition becomes a moment of revelation for the women, who now remember what Jesus said to them about rising from the dead. Having entered the empty tomb and been reminded of Jesus' words, the women understand the significance of the empty tomb: the tomb is empty because Jesus has risen from the dead as he promised. The women are now identified for the first time as Mary Magdalene, Joanna, Mary the mother of James, and the others who ministered to Jesus and the apostles when he was in Galilee (24:10; see 8:3). Although they tell their good news to the apostles, the apostles do not believe them. Peter, however, goes to the tomb. He is amazed, but he does not believe because he has not remembered Jesus' words that he must suffer, die, and rise.

Luke's carefully written account of the empty tomb highlights the need for interpretation. Of itself, the empty tomb does not bring the women or Peter to faith. But when the two men (angels) remind the women of Jesus' words, the remembrance of his words brings the women to faith, just as in the next episode Jesus' words will bring the two disciples to faith in the resurrection.

### *An Appearance to Two Disciples*

The story of the two disciples on their way to Emmaus, which follows the account of the empty tomb, is peculiar to Luke's gospel, although there is an echo of it in the longer ending of Mark's gospel (Mark 16:12-13). But whereas in Mark's story the disciples do not believe what the two disciples report, in Luke's gospel they believe because the Lord has already appeared to Peter (Luke 24:34).

Luke's story is artfully composed. We are told the name of one of the disciples, Cleopas, but not of the other. Jesus walks and talks with them, but they do not recognize him since "their eyes were kept from recognizing him" (24:16), a remark that echoes an earlier comment in the gospel when the disciples could not understand Jesus' passion prediction because "its meaning was concealed from them, so that they could not perceive it" (9:45). The risen Lord asks them what they are discussing, and they recount what has recently happened in Jerusalem. Although they were hoping that Jesus of Nazareth would be the one to redeem Israel, the recent events in Jerusalem have convinced them that even though Jesus was "a prophet mighty in deed and word before God and all the people" (24:19), he was not the redeemer they expected since he had been put to death.

Finally, the two disciples recap the story of the empty tomb. In their retelling of it, they now identify the two men at the tomb as angels, and they now relate that *several* of their number—not just Peter—went to the tomb. But even though they found the tomb empty, as the women reported, they did not see Jesus. Since there is no mention of faith here, we can suppose that those who visited the tomb were amazed by what they found, but they did not yet believe in the resurrection, another indication that the empty tomb itself does not lead to faith.

It is at this point in the narrative that Jesus reprimands the two for being foolish and slow to believe all that the prophets spoke. And just as the two men reminded the women of what the Son of Man said when he was among them, so the risen Lord interprets the Scriptures for them, explaining that what Moses and the prophets wrote referred to him.

Although the risen Lord has interpreted the meaning of the Scriptures for the two disciples, there is still no indication that they believe. One more step is needed. After they urge him to stay with them, he takes bread, breaks it, blesses it, and gives it to them, just as he did when he fed the five thousand (9:16) and when he established the new covenant at the Last Supper (22:19-23). Finally, their eyes are opened, and they recognize the stranger as the risen one. As soon as they do, however, he vanishes from their midst.

When the two return to Jerusalem to tell the eleven apostles that the Lord is risen, the eleven proclaim that the Lord is truly risen, for he has appeared to Simon. Only then are the two allowed to explain how they encountered the risen one in the breaking of the bread.

The account of the two disciples on the road to Emmaus makes several points. First, it is possible to be in the presence of the risen Christ, converse with him, and still not recognize him. Second, to believe in the resurrection, one must understand that Moses and the prophets had spoken about the Christ. Third, the risen Lord is present to the community of his disciples in the breaking of the bread. This presence, however, is elusive. For, while believers encounter him in Word and sacrament, they cannot control his presence.

### An Appearance to All of the Disciples

The appearances of the risen Lord to Simon/Peter and the two disciples might lead one to suspect that the disciples' faith is firm. But when the risen one appears to all of them, they are startled and terrified because they think they are seeing a ghost—a mere phantom of Jesus, but not the real person they once knew. Accordingly, the risen one must show them his hands and his feet, which had been nailed to the cross, and he invites them to touch him and know that he is "flesh and bones," and not a phantom. As a final proof that it is truly Jesus—the human one they once knew—he eats a piece of fish in their midst.

After showing them that he is not a spirit without bodily substance, the risen Christ explains the Scriptures to the eleven just as he did to the two disciples on the road to Emmaus, revealing that everything Moses and the prophets wrote about him had to be fulfilled. Luke's remark in 24:45 ("Then he opened their minds to understand the scriptures") indicates that this christological reading of Scripture must be taught since it is not immediately apparent. Apart from this enlightenment, it is impossible to understand the christological meaning of Scripture.

After opening their minds to understand the meaning of the Scriptures about him, the risen one commissions his apostles: "Thus it is written, that the Messiah is to suffer and to rise from the dead on the third day, and that repentance and forgiveness of sins is to be proclaimed in his name to all nations, beginning from Jerusalem. You are witnesses of these things" (24:46-48). Henceforth the very disciples who refused to believe in the resurrection will be its chief witnesses, and the purpose of their witness will be to preach repentance for the forgiveness of sins, a task they will undertake in the Acts of the Apostles.

### The Ascension

Like the longer ending of Mark's gospel, the Gospel of Luke concludes with a brief account of the Lord's ascension that will be repeated in the Acts of the Apostles. This account of the ascension brings to a close Jesus' "exodus" about which he spoke with Moses and Elijah when he was transfigured (9:31) as well as the goal of his journey to Jerusalem that was announced in 9:51: "When the days drew near for him *to be taken up*, he set his face to go to Jerusalem." The ascension reveals that the risen one is the exalted one who now sits at God's right hand, from where he watches over and guides the church.

### The Meaning of the Lukan Resurrection Narrative

The Lukan resurrection narrative takes up themes with which we are already familiar from the Gospel of Mark and introduces new ones as well. Like the Gospel of Mark, it highlights the importance of the empty tomb for resurrection faith. And, like the longer ending of the Gospel of Mark, it recounts the difficulty the disciples experienced in believing in the resurrection. But, in addition to these familiar motifs, the Gospel of Luke introduces new themes.

First, it highlights the bodily dimension of Jesus' resurrection by recounting how he invited his disciples to touch his hands and feet, and how he ate in their midst. Second, although Jesus has been raised from the dead, his resurrection was not a mere resuscitation from the dead. The two disciples on the road to Emmaus walk and talk with him, but they do not recognize him until he reveals himself to them. The risen one quickly disappears from the two disciples on the road to Emmaus, and the eleven apostles think they are seeing a ghost. The risen Christ is Jesus of Nazareth, the one who was crucified. But he now enjoys a bodily existence that transcends the corporal existence with which human beings are familiar.

Luke's most important contribution to our understanding of the resurrection, however, is the manner in which he relates Jesus' death and resurrection to the Scriptures and the breaking of the bread. The risen Christ teaches his disciples that Moses and the prophets spoke about his death and resurrection, and he reveals himself to them in the breaking of the bread. Luke's emphasis on the christological meaning of Scripture and the breaking of the bread indicate that resurrection faith is possible for all whose minds have been opened to understand the christological meaning of Scripture and share in the community's eucharistic celebration.

## The Resurrection Narrative in the Gospel according to John

The resurrection narrative of the Gospel of John consists of a story of the empty tomb at which the risen Lord appears first to Mary Magdalene and then, on three other occasions, to his disciples. Three of the Lord's appearances occur in Jerusalem, the fourth and last in Galilee. The narrative unfolds in the following way. Mary Magdalene discovers the empty tomb. After Peter and the Beloved Disciple[12] visit the tomb, the risen Lord appears to Mary (20:1-18). That same day, in the evening, he also appears to all of the disciples except Thomas, who is absent (20:19-23). A week later, however, the risen Christ appears to the disciples again, and this time Thomas is present (20:24-29). Chapter 20 then concludes with what appears to be the ending of the gospel (20:30-31). But in the next chapter, the risen Lord appears a third time to seven of his disciples at the Sea of Tiberias, the Lake of Galilee (21:1-19). The gospel then ends with what seems to be a second conclusion (21:20-25).

### *The Empty Tomb and the Appearance to Mary Magdalene*

The Johannine account of the empty tomb is told in a new way. Mary Magdalene (there is no mention of any other women) comes to the tomb and discovers that the stone has been rolled away. There is no mention of Mary's intention to anoint the body, nor is there any vision of angels when she first arrives. Instead, Mary immediately tells Peter and the Beloved Disciple that someone has stolen the Lord's body. Although the Beloved Disciple arrives at the tomb before Peter, Peter is the first to enter the tomb, where he finds Jesus' burial clothing but not his body. Next, the Beloved Disciple enters the tomb, and the evangelist says that "he saw and believed" (20:8), thereby suggesting that the Beloved Disciple has understood the true meaning of the empty tomb. The remark that follows explains why Peter and Mary did not understand what the Beloved Disciple did: "for as yet they did not understand the scripture, that he must rise from the dead" (20:9).

Although the two disciples return home, Mary remains behind. Peering into the tomb, she sees two angels who ask why she is weeping. She, however, does not realize they are angels. After telling them that she is weeping because the body has been taken away and she does not know where it is, she turns around and sees the risen Lord (whom she mistakes for the gardener), who repeats the same question asked by the angels. It is only when the risen one, the Good Shepherd who calls his sheep by name (see 10:3-5), calls her by name, "Mary," that she recognizes it is Jesus. When she tries to hold on to him, the risen one tells her not to cling to him since he has not yet ascended to his Father.[13] She must, instead, tell his disciples that he is ascending to "my Father and your Father, to my God and your God" (20:18).

Like the Synoptic accounts, the Johannine gospel shows that the empty tomb is an essential part of the resurrection narrative inasmuch as it points to the bodily resurrection of Jesus. In the Johannine account, unlike the Synoptic accounts, however, there is one person (the Beloved Disciple) who seems to understand the significance of the empty tomb. Furthermore, Mary Magdalene plays an even more central role than she does in the other gospels. She is the first to see the risen Lord who, like a good shepherd, calls her by name, and she is the first to announce the resurrection to Jesus' disciples. Finally, Jesus' remark that he is about to ascend to his Father indicates that his resurrection is not a return to his former way of life but an entrance into a transcendent new life that Paul will describe in 1 Corinthians 15.

## *The First Appearance to the Disciples*

The gospel does not recount the reaction of the disciples to Mary's announcement that she has seen the Lord. But it does narrate the appearance of the Lord to his disciples that same evening. The focus of this account is the commissioning of the disciples. The Lord appears to them with the greeting, "Peace be with you" (20:19). He then repeats this greeting and commissions them: "As the Father has sent me, so I send you" (20:21). This commission echoes a major theme of the Johannine gospel: Just as the Father sent the Son into the world to reveal to the world what he has seen and heard in the presence of the Father, so Jesus sends his disciples into the world to reveal to the world what the Son has revealed to them. To enable the disciples to complete their mission, Jesus breathes the Spirit upon them and empowers them to forgive the sins of others since he is the Lamb of God who has taken away the sin of the world (1:29). This narrative has two interesting affinities with the conclusion of Luke's gospel in which (1) the risen one tells the disciples that they must preach repentance for the forgiveness of sins and (2) they will receive the promise of the Father, namely, the Holy Spirit (Luke 24:46-48).

## *The Second Appearance to the Disciples*

It is only at the beginning of the next story that we are told that Thomas, one of the Twelve, was not present when Jesus appeared (20:24). This allows the evangelist to present Thomas as someone who refuses to believe unless he has first seen the risen Lord and to assure those who have not seen the risen one, "Blessed are those who have not seen and yet have come to believe" (20:29).

The episode occurs a week later, while the disciples are in Jerusalem, presumably after the risen one has ascended to his Father, although this is not mentioned. Thomas's insistence that he touch the hands and side of the Lord, and the risen Lord's invitation to do so, provides the gospel's audience with further assurance of the bodily nature of the Lord's resurrection.[14] The risen one is not a ghost (Luke 24:27); he is the same Jesus they once knew, although he is now glorified. Recognizing that the risen one is the crucified one whom the Father has glorified, Thomas confirms the Christology that occurs throughout this gospel by proclaiming that Jesus is his Lord and his God.

## The Third Appearance to the Disciples

Although the ending of chapter 20 gives the impression that the gospel ends at this point (20:30-31), the opening verse of chapter 21 provides a smooth transition from the first two appearances of Jesus to his disciples to a third: "After these things *Jesus showed himself again* to the disciples by the Sea of Tiberias; and he showed himself in this way" (21:1). This third and final appearance occurs in Galilee before seven of Jesus' disciples: Simon Peter, Thomas, Nathaniel, Zebedee's sons (James and John), and two others, one of whom is later identified as the Beloved Disciple (21:20). The appearance unfolds in three acts, each with its own motif: the risen Lord appears to the seven disciples while they are fishing (21:1-14), the risen Lord commissions Peter to feed his flock (21:15-19), and the risen Lord speaks of what will happen to the Beloved Disciple (21:20-23).

The first part of the narrative contains a missionary and eucharistic motif. The disciples have been fishing all night and caught nothing. Accordingly, when the risen Lord appears to them on the shore (although they do not recognize him at first), he instructs them to cast their nets on the right side of the boat. They then draw in an immense catch of 153 fish that does not tear their nets.[15] This great catch points to the fruitful mission that lies ahead for the disciples. From now on, they will catch human beings whom they will hold in the unity of a net that will not break, a community that finds its unity in the risen Lord.

In the second part of the narrative, the risen Lord reconciles Peter, who had denied him three times, by asking him three times if he loves him. After each of Peter's three responses, the Lord instructs him to feed his flock. He then indicates that Peter will die in the same way that he did, thereby glorifying God by his death as did Jesus. At the end of this scene, the risen Lord summons Peter to follow him once more.

Finally, in response to a question by Peter about the fate of the Beloved Disciple, the risen Lord gives a cryptic answer: "If it is my

will that he remain until I come, what is that to you? Follow me"
(21:22). Jesus' response to Peter is one of the few times in the Fourth
Gospel that he speaks about his return at the end of the ages in language similar to the Synoptic Gospels. In doing so, the Johannine
Jesus makes a connection between his resurrection and his return
at the end of the ages, as does Paul.

## The Meaning of the Johannine Resurrection Narrative

While the Johannine narrative echoes the accounts of Matthew,
Mark, and Luke, it introduces new stories and themes not found in
the Synoptic Gospels, most notably the appearance to Thomas and
the appearance to the seven in Galilee. Like the Synoptic Gospels,
the Johannine narrative begins with an account of the empty tomb
and then proceeds to recount a number of stories in which the risen
Christ appears first to Mary, and then to his disciples. The Johannine
narrative, however, relates these stories in a way that coheres with its
overall theology of Jesus' mission. Just as the Father sent Jesus into
the world to reveal what he has seen and heard in the Father' presence, so the risen Christ sends his disciples into the world to reveal
what they have seen and heard in his presence about the Father. For
the Johannine gospel, the resurrection is the origin of the church's
mission, the moment when the church must do what Jesus has done.

## Conclusion

A close reading of the way in which the four gospels relate the
story of Jesus' resurrection indicates that the events they narrate
should not be harmonized. They do not agree about the names of
the women who visited the tomb, what happened at the tomb, or
the number and kind of appearances of the risen Lord. However,
they do concur on some important matters. For example, the stone
had been removed from the tomb and the tomb was empty. Women
were the first to discover the empty tomb. The meaning of the empty
tomb, however, is not immediately self-evident; its meaning needs
to be interpreted by others and by Scripture. The risen Lord appears
to a variety of people both in Jerusalem and Galilee. But even those

to whom he appears do not immediately recognize him or understand the full significance of his appearance to them. Accordingly, the risen one assures them that it is truly he. Finally, the appearance of the risen one leads to mission. Those to whom he appears must proclaim the good news of his resurrection to others.

Despite their differences, the gospel narratives tend to emphasize two points. First, by raising Jesus from the dead, God vindicated Jesus, confirming his proclamation of the kingdom of God and his claim to be the one whom the Father sent into the world to reveal the Father to the world. Second, the resurrection of Jesus becomes the occasion for the risen Lord to send his disciples on a mission and proclaim the message of the kingdom and the revelation he brings from the Father. Both of these topics (the vindication of Jesus and the mission of the disciples) play a major role in the material from the Acts of the Apostles that I will investigate in the next chapter.

## Notes

1. For a helpful defense of the historicity of the resurrection narratives, see Gerald O'Collins, SJ, *Believing in the Resurrection: The Meaning and Promise of the Risen Jesus* (New York: Paulist Press, 2012).

2. For example, see the older but still helpful works of Reginald H. Fuller, *The Formation of the Resurrection Narratives* (New York: Macmillan, 1971), and Norman Perrin, *The Resurrection according to Matthew, Mark, and Luke* (Philadelphia: Fortress, 1977).

3. For a careful narrative approach to the resurrection narratives, see Francis J. Moloney, SDB, *The Resurrection of the Messiah: A Narrative Commentary on the Resurrection Accounts in the Four Gospels* (New York: Paulist Press, 2013).

4. The earliest attempt to describe this event is found in the apocryphal Gospel of Peter 10:38: "When those soldiers saw this, they awakened the centurion and the elders, for they also were there to mount guard. And while they were narrating what they had seen, they saw three men come out from the sepulcher, two of them supporting the other and a cross

followed them and the heads of the two reaching to heaven, but that of him who was being led reached beyond the heavens. And they heard a voice out of the heavens crying, 'Have you preached to those who sleep?', and from the cross there was heard the answer, 'Yes.'" Quoted from J. K. Elliott, ed., *The Apocryphal New Testament: A Collection of Apocryphal Literature in an English Translation based on M. R. James* (Oxford: Clarendon Press, 1993), 156–57.

5. An attempt at a description of the risen Christ, which I will discuss in chapter 5, is found in the first chapter of the book of Revelation.

6. There are actually four endings to the Gospel of Mark in the manuscript tradition. (1) Mark 16:1-8 is found in the oldest and best manuscripts. (2) Mark 16:9-20 is the longest ending, but it is absent from the two best Greek manuscripts (Vaticanus and Sinaiticus). Clement of Alexandria and Origen were not aware of this ending. This ending, however, is received as canonical by the Catholic Church. (3) This longer ending also circulates in some manuscripts with a further verse after 16:14. Since this verse is found in the Washington Codex, which is housed in the Freer Gallery in Washington, DC, it is called the Freer Logion. (4) Some manuscripts witness to a shorter ending between 16:1-8 and 16:9-20, but this ending is not assigned a verse number.

7. Christopher Bryan (*The Resurrection of the Messiah* [New York: Oxford University Press, 2011]) is a representative of this approach. He writes, "The women did not rush out and immediately start chattering to everyone, thereby disobeying the angel's command that they go to the disciples with their news: rather, they fled the angel's presence in silence, greeting no one by the way, for they were filled with awe by both message and messenger" (79). He also notes, "Moreover, if it *were* not conveyed, it would mean that at the last moment attention was directed away from the mystery of the resurrection to the feelings of the women, which is, surely, the last thing that Mark would have intended" (80).

8. Francis J. Moloney (*The Resurrection of the Messiah*) is representative of this approach: "The explanation of the enigma of the failure of the women in 16:8 lies in Mark's desire to instruct his readers/listeners that the encounter between the risen Jesus and his failed disciples did not take place because of the success of the women. As the disciples failed (14:50-52), so also the women failed (16:8). In the end, *all human beings fail . . . but God succeeds*" (16).

9. Geert Van Oyen ("The Empty Tomb Story in Mark," in *Resurrection of the Dead: Biblical Traditions in Dialogue*, BETL 249 [Leuven: Peeters,

2012]) is representative of this approach: "The story demands continuation, but as there is no sequel for and by the characters within the story, only one person is left to do what the women did not do: the reader" (146).

10. The gospel both begins and ends in Jerusalem, and Jesus' decision to journey to Jerusalem (9:51) is a major turning point in the gospel.

11. In Luke's gospel, the story of a woman anointing Jesus occurs earlier, during Jesus' ministry in Galilee (8:36-50). It is not related in the Passion narrative as it is in the gospels of Matthew and Mark.

12. The Beloved Disciple refers to a disciple who appears often in the gospel narrative but is never identified apart from being called the disciple whom Jesus loved. He is clearly the authoritative witness that stands behind this gospel.

13. This remark does not mean that Mary will be able to touch him after he has ascended, but that he has entered into a new sphere of being that is different from his former relationship with her. Therefore, she must not hold on to or cling to her former relationship with him but learn to relate to him in a new way.

14. There is no tension between this invitation to touch his wounds and the rebuke to Mary because the purpose of each story is different. Whereas Mary wants to cling to her old relationship with Jesus, Thomas needs to be shown that the resurrected one is the crucified one.

15. Although Origen proposed that the number refers to all the known species of fish and others have proposed symbolic meanings for the number 153, there is no agreement about the meaning of the number.

# Chapter 3

# The Witness of
# the Acts of the Apostles

In the previous chapter, I examined the different ways in which the gospels present Jesus' resurrection from the dead. While they differ in how they recount the resurrection, all of them begin with an account of the empty tomb before narrating how the risen Lord appeared to certain women and his disciples. The purpose of these appearance stories is twofold. First, they explain the significance of the empty tomb. Second, they recount how the risen Lord reconstituted the community of his disciples and commissioned them to proclaim the gospel to the world. Thus the Lord's resurrection has a profound missionary component. Those to whom the risen Lord appears must preach the good news of the kingdom that Jesus proclaimed. Their proclamation of the kingdom, however, has a new component since *the one who proclaimed the kingdom has entered into the fullness of the kingdom*. For, by raising Jesus from the dead, God vindicated the gospel of the kingdom that Jesus preached and brought him into the fullness of the kingdom. Consequently, to proclaim the resurrection is to proclaim the kingdom, and to proclaim the kingdom is to proclaim the resurrection. Understood in this sense, it is correct to say that *the one who proclaimed the kingdom has become the content of the church's preaching.*

The Acts of the Apostles is the next logical step in our investigation of the resurrection since it provides us with the most detailed account we possess of how the early church announced the gospel by proclaiming the resurrection of Jesus. Acts, to be sure, is not a history of the early church in the way we understand history today. Luke (who is also the author of the gospel that bears his name) describes the purpose of his two-volume work in this way: "I too decided, after investigating everything carefully from the very first, to write an orderly account for you, most excellent Theophilus, so that you may know the truth concerning the things about which you have been instructed" (Luke 1:3-4). Like a good historian, Luke has investigated the sources anew, but his purpose is not merely to write history; *he writes to strengthen the faith of those who already believe.* Given the nature of Luke's work, we will not find a dispassionate history of the early church so much as we will discover a narrative that proclaims the gospel by highlighting God's redemptive purpose in the life and ministry of Jesus and of the early church that proclaimed his resurrection.

While the whole of Acts provides a witness to the resurrection, it is the speeches of Acts that do most of the work, especially those of Peter and Paul. Accordingly, after describing the appearances of the risen Lord to the eleven apostles and then to Paul, this chapter focuses on the witness of Peter to the resurrection in the sermons and speeches he delivers at Pentecost, in the temple of Jerusalem, before the Sanhedrin, and to the household of Cornelius. It then turns to Paul's witness to the resurrection as found in his sermons at Antioch in Pisidia, Athens, and the defense speeches he delivers in Jerusalem and Caesarea.

## The Appearances of the Risen Lord in Acts

The Acts of the Apostles narrates two kinds of appearances by the risen Lord: appearances over a period of forty days to the eleven apostles and appearances to Paul, the most important being his call to be the Lord's chosen instrument to bring his name to Gentiles, kings, and Israelites (9:15). Since these appearances are foundational for the preaching of Paul and the apostles, I begin with them.

### *The Appearances to the Eleven*

Luke opens his account of the early church by recapitulating what he has written. He says that in his first volume (the gospel) he dealt with all that Jesus said and did until the day he was taken up into heaven. He then notes that Jesus "presented himself alive to them by many convincing proofs, appearing to them during forty days and speaking about the kingdom of God" (1:3). But whereas in the gospel Luke recounts these appearances at length, in the Acts of the Apostles he simply mentions them, noting that (1) Jesus appeared to the eleven (2) during a period of forty days, (3) showing them by many convincing proofs that he was truly alive, and (4) speaking to them about the kingdom of God. The purpose of these appearances becomes apparent when Jesus tells the eleven apostles that they will be his *witnesses* in Jerusalem, throughout Judea and Samaria, and to the ends of the earth (1:8). From this verse it is clear that Jesus appears to the eleven over a period of forty days, presenting himself as risen and alive, so that they will be qualified to witness to his resurrection. By appearing to them and speaking to them about the kingdom of God—the central message of the gospel—the risen Lord leaves no room for doubt that he is the one who proclaimed the kingdom of God during his earthly ministry. Accordingly, the primary task of the apostles after they have received power from on high will be to witness to the resurrection, a task for which the risen Lord has prepared them.

Shortly after Jesus is taken up into heaven, Peter gathers the community of believers in Jerusalem to find a replacement for Judas so that the twelve apostles, who will be the rulers of a renewed Israel, can call Israel to repentance by witnessing to the resurrection. In specifying the requirements for Judas's replacement, Peter says, "So one of the men who have accompanied us during all the time that the Lord Jesus went in and out among us, beginning from the baptism of John until the day when he was taken up from us—*one of these must become a witness with us to his resurrection*" (1:21-22). The one who will take Judas's place must be someone who can witness to the Lord's whole career from the beginning of his ministry to the day of his ascension, thereby witnessing to the continuity between the earthly Jesus and the risen Lord. The manner in which Acts begins leaves no doubt that the primary task of the reconstituted Twelve will be to witness to the resurrection.

### The Appearances to Paul

Just as the risen Christ appeared to the apostles in order to prepare them to witness to his resurrection, so he appeared to Paul. The appearances of the risen Lord to Paul, however, are of a different kind insofar as they occur after the ascension, the period during which Jesus is enthroned in heaven as God's Messiah, according to Luke (see Acts 2:33). To be sure, the same Lord appears to both Paul and the apostles. But whereas the apostles see the risen Christ in a bodily form that highlights the continuity between the earthly Jesus and the risen Christ, Paul encounters the ascended and enthroned Lord in a glorious light that blinds him.

The most important text is the account of Paul's call/conversion that Luke recounts in Acts 9, which Paul later retells from his own point of view in Acts 22 and 26. In Acts 9 the risen Lord appears to Paul in a light from heaven that flashes around him, and a voice calls, "Saul, Saul, why do you persecute me?" (9:4). When Paul asks who is speaking, the risen Lord replies, "I am Jesus, whom you are persecuting" (9:5).While those traveling with Paul hear the voice, they do not see the risen Lord as Paul did. Paul, however, is blinded by the light he has seen, which is the glory of the risen Lord, and must be led by the hand into Damascus, where the Lord has already appeared in a vision to a disciple named Ananias and designated Paul as his chosen instrument. After Ananias tells Paul that it is Jesus who appeared to him, Paul regains his sight, is baptized, and begins to preach that Jesus is the Son of God, the Messiah (9:20, 22).

Later in Acts, Paul recounts the narrative of Acts 9 from his point of view. In Acts 22 he says, "about noon a great light from heaven suddenly shone about me" (22:6). When Paul asks who is speaking to him, the voice replies, "I am Jesus of Nazareth whom you are persecuting" (22:8). Paul then meets Ananias, whom he describes as "a devout man according to the law and well spoken of by all the Jews living there" (22:12). It is Ananias who tells Paul that it is the God of Israel's ancestors who designated him to "know his will, to see the Righteous One," and to hear the sound of his voice since Paul "will be his witness to all the world of what you have seen and heard" (22:14, 15).

In addition to narrating his call in chapter 22, Paul recounts a vision of the risen Lord that occurred when he fell into a trance while praying in the temple of Jerusalem (22:17-21). During that trance he saw the Lord, but he does not describe what he saw. A conversation follows between Paul and the Lord at the end of which the Lord sends Paul to preach to the Gentiles.

Paul recounts his call a second time in chapter 26. This time he describes what he saw as "a light from heaven, brighter than the sun, shining around me and my companions" (26:13). The voice that he hears speaks in Hebrew, saying, "Saul, Saul, why are you persecuting me? It hurts you to kick against the goads" (26:14). Once more the risen Lord identifies himself as Jesus, whom Paul is persecuting. But in this account, there is no mention of Ananias. Instead, it is the risen Lord who commissions Paul directly:

> But get up and stand on your feet; for I have appeared to you for this purpose, to appoint you to serve and testify to the things in which you have seen me and to those in which I will appear to you. I will rescue you from your people and from the Gentiles—to whom I am sending you to open their eyes so that they may turn from darkness to light and from the power of Satan to God, so that they may receive forgiveness of sins and a place among those who are sanctified by faith in me. (26:16-18)

The risen Lord's appearances to Paul are similar to and different from his appearances to the apostles. Whereas the risen Christ appears to the eleven apostles in a bodily form that is familiar to them because they knew the earthly Jesus, the enthroned Christ appears to Paul in radiant light that points to his resurrection glory. In both instances, however, the purpose of these appearances is the same: to make Paul and the apostles witnesses to the resurrection of Jesus. After these appearances, the apostle and Paul can preach with boldness that Jesus is the Messiah because they know from personal experience that Jesus is risen and alive.

## Peter's Witness to the Resurrection

Before he was taken up into heaven, the risen Lord instructed his apostles to remain in Jerusalem until they received the promise of the Father, namely, the Holy Spirit (Luke 24:49; Acts 1:4). It was this gift of the Spirit that descended upon the early community at Pentecost and enabled the apostles to witness to the resurrection in a powerful way that confounded those who opposed them. The first example of this is Peter's speech on Pentecost (2:14-36).

### Peter's Witness at Pentecost

The occasion for this speech is the Spirit-empowered speaking of the apostles at Pentecost that enables them to speak in other languages. Bewildered by this, some accuse the apostles of being drunk. In response to this charge, Peter begins his speech with an extended quotation from the prophet Joel to show that the outpouring of the Spirit is the fulfillment of prophecy (2:14-21). Although he was not trained in the interpretation of the Scriptures, Peter has become a skilled interpreter of them because the risen Christ has revealed what was written about him in the Prophets and the Psalms (Luke 24:46). Peter has received the promise of the Father, the gift of the Spirit of God that enables him to interpret Scripture in light of the resurrection.

Next, Peter summarizes the central events of Jesus' ministry to the assembled crowd of Jerusalemites whom he addresses as Israelites (2:22-24). God confirmed Jesus' ministry among them through a series of mighty deeds performed through Jesus. Despite these mighty deeds, they handed Jesus over to be crucified. Contrasting what they did and what God did, Peter affirms that God raised Jesus from the dead:

> [T]his man, handed over to you according to the definite plan and foreknowledge of God, *you crucified and killed by the hands of those outside the law. But God raised him up, having freed him from death,* because it was impossible for him to be held in its power. (2:23-24)

This strong contrast formula, which we will meet again, affirms that the resurrection was an act of God, who vindicated Jesus by raising him from the dead.

Next, Peter employs two texts from the Psalms that he interprets in light of Jesus' resurrection (2:25-36). First, he quotes Psalm 16:8-11, which he attributes to David:

> For David says concerning him,
>     "I saw the Lord always before me,
>         for he is at my right hand so that I will not be shaken;
>     therefore my heart was glad,
>         and my tongue rejoiced;
>         moreover my flesh will live in hope.
>     *For you will not abandon my soul to Hades,*
>         *or let your Holy One experience corruption.*
>     You have made known to me the ways of life;
>         you will make me full of gladness with your presence."
>             (Acts 2:25-28)

Peter has become a skilled interpreter of Scripture. He notes that David died and was buried, and that his tomb is still in their midst (2:29). Therefore, the promise that God would not abandon the soul of his Holy One to Hades or let him see corruption cannot apply to David, the author of the psalm. Rather, speaking as a prophet, David must have had someone else in view: namely, Jesus the Messiah whom God raised from the dead.

Peter goes on to provide a second proof from prophecy, this time from Psalm 110:1:

> The Lord said to my Lord,
> "Sit at my right hand,
>     until I make your enemies
>         your footstool." (Acts 2:34-35)

Here again Peter argues that this psalm cannot apply to David since David did not ascend to heaven. Therefore, it must refer to another, namely, to Jesus whom God raised from the dead. On the basis of his proof from prophecy, Peter concludes, "Therefore let the entire house of Israel know with certainty that God has made him both Lord and Messiah, this Jesus whom you crucified" (2:36). For Peter, the resurrection is the proof that God has made Jesus "Lord and Messiah" despite the ignominy of his crucifixion—for by raising Jesus from the dead, God has enthroned him at his right as Messiah and Lord.

### Peter's Witness in the Temple

The healing of a paralytic in the temple (3:1-10) is the occasion for Peter's second sermon in which he witnesses to the Lord's resurrection (3:11-26). When a great crowd assembles, amazed at this healing, Peter launches into his sermon. In the first part he employs an extended contrast formula to explain that he did not perform this mighty deed by his own power. It was by faith in the name of Jesus, whom the God of their ancestors glorified by raising him from the dead after they had handed him over and denied him in the presence of Pilate (3:11-16). This extended contrast formula, which contrasts what God did with what they did, can be summarized in this way:

> The *God* of their ancestors glorified his servant Jesus whom
> > *They* handed over and denied
> > *They* denied the holy and righteous one and asked for a murderer
> > *They* put the author of life to death
> But *God* raised him from the dead

Having seen the risen Lord over a period of forty days, Peter and the other apostles understand that the God of Israel vindicated Jesus by raising him from the dead. In light of the resurrection, Peter perceives that Jesus was God's servant, the holy and righteous one, the author of life. Inasmuch as he was the first whom God raised from the dead, Jesus brings resurrection life to those who believe in him.

In the second part of his sermon (3:17-26) Peter tempers his condemnation of the crowd by acknowledging that they and their leaders acted in ignorance of God's plan, which the prophets had already announced, and he calls the crowd to conversion. In denying the holy and righteous one and in putting the author of life to death, they unwittingly fulfilled what the prophets foretold, namely, that the Messiah would suffer. This Messiah is Jesus, who is now enthroned in heaven until the appointed time of universal restoration (3:21).

Reminding the crowd that Moses promised that God would raise up a prophet like himself and that everyone who does not listen to this prophet will be cut off from the people (Deut 18:15), Peter concludes his sermon by instructing the crowd it was for them first of all, the people of Israel, that God raised up his servant Jesus to bless them and turn them from their sins.

Peter's witness to the resurrection makes several points. First, the resurrection was God's act of glorifying his servant Jesus whom human beings rejected. Second, by the resurrection Jesus has become the author of life—resurrection life—for all who believe in his name. Third, the resurrection authenticates Jesus as God's Messiah. Fourth, the risen Messiah is the enthroned Messiah who is in heaven waiting for the day appointed by God when he will return and restore all things.

### Peter's Witness before the Religious Authorities

Just as Jesus' temple ministry brought him into conflict with the religious authorities in Jerusalem, so Peter's witness to the resurrection in the temple brings him and the other apostles into conflict with the religious authorities of Jerusalem. The priests, the captain of the temple, and the Sadducees are disturbed that Peter and John were "teaching the people and proclaiming that *in Jesus there is the resurrection of the dead*" (Acts 4:2). Given that the Sadducees, unlike the Pharisees, did not believe that there would be a resurrection of the dead, the teaching of Peter and John is a threat to their position as those charged to teach the people of Israel. Accordingly, the next day the apostles are summoned before the Sanhedrin and asked by what authority they are doing what they are doing, the same question they asked Jesus when he taught in the temple (Luke 20:2).

Peter's response is not so much a sermon as it is an accusation against the religious leaders. There is no acknowledgment that they acted in ignorance, nor is there any call for them to repent. As in his sermons at Pentecost and in the temple, Peter employs a contrast formula to reinforce how God vindicated Jesus by reversing what the leaders did. Luke introduces Peter's speech by noting that he was "filled with the Holy Spirit" (4:8), just as Jesus promised his disciples they would be (Luke 12:11-12), thereby alerting readers of his account that Peter's defense has been inspired by the Spirit of God. As in his temple speech, Peter takes no credit for the mighty deed that occurred in the temple. What happened there occurred through the name of Jesus the Nazorean whom *they crucified* but *God raised from the dead* (4:11). Inspired by the Spirit, Peter once more proves to be a skilled interpreter of Scripture by identifying Jesus as the stone rejected by them, the builders. Although Peter does not explicitly quote from Scripture, the biblically literate reader hears an allusion to Psalm 118:22: "The stone that the builders rejected / has become the chief cornerstone." Inspired by the Spirit, Peter and the early church are beginning to read Scripture in light of the resurrection. In this case, the rejected stone is the crucified Jesus who has become the cornerstone of God's eschatological temple in virtue of his being raised from the dead.

Amazed by the boldness with which Peter and John speak, even though they are uneducated men, the Sanhedrin forbids them from speaking further "in the name of Jesus" (4:18), to which the apostles reply, "Whether it is right in God's sight to listen to you rather than to God, you must judge; for we cannot keep from speaking about what we have seen and heard" (4:19-20). What the apostles have *seen and heard* is the risen Lord who appeared and spoke to them over a period of forty days, showing them in many convincing ways that he is truly risen and alive. For the apostles to stop speaking in the name of Jesus would require them to cease witnessing to the resurrection of Jesus, of which they are now fully convinced.

Because Peter and John and all of the apostles refuse to stop speaking in the name of Jesus, all of them are arrested and summoned before the Sanhedrin. When the religious leaders remind them of the strict orders they gave to them, Peter *and all of the apostles* witness anew to the resurrection (5:29-32). Their brief defense makes three points. First, they must obey God rather than human beings. Second, God has reversed what they, the leaders of Israel, did: *They* killed Jesus by having him crucified, but *God* raised him from the dead, exalting him at his right hand as leader and savior of Israel for the forgiveness of sins. Third, they and the Holy Spirit are witnesses to these things.

Although brief, this defense reveals a growing understanding of the resurrection. The resurrection was an act whereby God exalted the crucified Jesus at his right hand, thereby establishing him in power and authority. As the exalted Messiah, the risen Christ—not the religious leaders who condemned him—has become the leader and savior of the people. For Peter and the apostles it is no longer possible to stop witnessing to the resurrection. They now see with perfect clarity how God has exalted the crucified Jesus by raising him from the dead.

### Peter's Witness to Gentiles

The final speech in which Peter explicitly bears witness to the resurrection occurs in the longest story of Acts, the conversion of the household of Cornelius (10:1–11:18). This narrative is a major turning point in Acts since it justifies preaching the gospel to Gentiles as well as to Jews.

Peter's sermon (10:34-43) occurs in the middle of this episode, after he has arrived at the household of Cornelius. His opening remarks indicate that he has come to a fuller understanding of God and of the gospel that, to this point, he has only preached to Jews. Having been instructed by the Spirit to go to Cornelius's house, Peter now understands that "God shows no partiality" since all who fear him and do what he requires, no matter what their national origin, are acceptable to him (10:34-35).

After acknowledging his new understanding of God's impartiality, Peter summarizes the main events of Jesus' public ministry as he did in his sermon at Pentecost (10:36-39). But in this summary of Jesus' ministry, he now refers to Jesus Christ as the one who is "Lord of all," thereby indicating that the risen Lord is more than the Jewish Messiah. In virtue of his resurrection, by which he has been exalted at God's right hand, the risen Christ has become the Lord of the Gentiles as well as of the people of Israel.

As in his other speeches, Peter introduces a strong contrast formula between what human beings did and what God has done: *they* put him to death by crucifying him, *but God* raised him on the third day and allowed him to appear, not to everybody, but to witnesses chosen in advance who ate and drank with him after his resurrection, commissioning them to preach that he is the one whom God has appointed to judge the living and the dead (10:39-42). Speaking to Gentiles who know something of the Jewish Scriptures, Peter concludes that all of the prophets bear witness to the risen Lord (10:43).

While this sermon echoes many of the themes of earlier speeches and sermons, it introduces new themes and presents familiar themes in another way. For example, by calling Jesus Christ "the Lord of all," this sermon indicates that God's act of raising Jesus from the dead is intended for Gentiles as well as for Jews. And by noting that God allowed the risen Christ to appear to chosen witnesses with whom he ate and drank, this sermon highlights the transcendent as well as the corporeal nature of the resurrection. On the one hand, the risen one can only be seen by those to whom God allows him to appear. On the other, the risen Lord who has entered into a new sphere of being remains the crucified Jesus.

The speeches and sermons that Peter delivers in Acts make the following points. First, the resurrection was a powerful act of God whereby God vindicated Jesus of Nazareth by raising him from the dead. Second, the resurrection of Jesus is confirmed by the Law, the Psalms, and the Prophets. Third, the risen Lord appeared in a bodily way to chosen witnesses over an extended period of time to show them that he was truly risen and alive. Fourth, by the resurrection God glorified and exalted the crucified Jesus, as Lord and Messiah. Fifth, the risen Christ is presently enthroned as the Messiah who is waiting to return on the day of universal resurrection. Sixth, God raised Jesus from the dead to bring Jews and Gentiles to repentance for the forgiveness of sins. Seventh, the apostles are witnesses whom God chose in advance to proclaim that the crucified Jesus has been raised from the dead.

## Paul's Witness to the Resurrection

Whereas Peter and the apostles are the primary witnesses to the resurrection in the first half of the Acts of the Apostles, it is Paul who is the dominant witness in the second half of Acts. Although we can suppose that Paul witnessed to the resurrection whenever he preached about Christ and the kingdom of God, there are certain speeches and sermons in which his witness is more explicit: his sermon in the synagogue of Antioch in Pisidia, his speech at Athens, and a number of speeches he delivers in Jerusalem and Caesarea in which he must defend himself against the charge that he leads the people of Israel astray.

## Paul's Witness in Antioch of Pisidia

Paul's sermon in the synagogue of Antioch of Pisidia (13:16-41), which he delivers during the course of his first missionary journey, provides us with an example of how he preached to Jews and God-fearers in synagogues. He begins with an account of Israel's history, highlighting certain events from the time of the patriarchs to the time of John the Baptist (13:17-25). He then draws out the implications of that history for his audience, providing listeners with proof from Scripture that the promises made to their ancestors have been fulfilled in Jesus' resurrection from the dead (13:26-41).

Paul's review of Israel's history begins with the election of their ancestors whom God delivered from the land of Egypt. It recounts their wandering in the wilderness, their conquest of the land of Canaan, the period of the judges, and the establishment of the monarchy. It says nothing, however, about the Assyrian deportation, the exile, or the period following the exile. Paul is primarily interested in the promise God made to David that he would bring forth a savior from David's descendants. This savior is the one whom John the Baptist announced.

Having shown his audience that the whole of their history finds its culmination in Jesus, who is David's descendant, in the second part of his sermon Paul explains the significance of the events that have recently transpired in Jerusalem. The inhabitants of that city did not recognize that Jesus was the promised savior, and so they asked Pilate to put him to death. "But God raised him from the dead" (13:30). The risen Jesus appeared over the course of several days to those who accompanied him from Galilee to Jerusalem, and they now witness that God raised him from the dead.

It is at this point in his sermon that Paul draws a connection between the promises God made to their ancestors and the resurrection of Jesus: "And we bring you the good news that what God promised to our ancestors he has fulfilled for us, their children, by raising Jesus; as also it is written in the second psalm, / 'You are my Son; / today I have begotten you'" (13:32-33). With this statement it is clear that the promises God made to Israel have found their fulfillment in the resurrection of the Messiah.

Next, Paul provides his audience with a series of scriptural proofs to convince them that Jesus' resurrection is the culmination of the promise God made to their ancestors. The first of these proofs is from Psalm 2, a psalm that was sung in the presence of the newly anointed king on the day of his coronation. Paul and the early church, however, now understand this psalm in light of Jesus' resurrection. The "today" to which the psalm refers is the day of the resurrection; it is the day on which God begot Jesus as his Son by enthroning him in power.

Drawing next on Psalm 16, Paul employs the same scriptural argument that Peter used in his sermon at Pentecost. The psalm as quoted in Acts 13:35 reads, "You will not let your Holy One experience corruption." Like Peter, Paul notes that since David died and his body suffered corruption this psalm must refer to someone else, namely, Jesus, the one whose body did not see corruption since God raised him from the dead. The sermon, as related by Luke, concludes with a nod to Paul's teaching on justification by faith: "Let it be known to you therefore, my brothers, that through this man forgiveness of sins is proclaimed to you; by this Jesus everyone who believes is set free from all those sins from which you could not be freed by the law of Moses" (13:38-39).

This carefully crafted sermon echoes familiar motifs from Peter's sermons, for example, the contrast between what human beings did and what God has done, the witness of the apostles to the resurrection, and the use of Psalm 16. But it also introduces a new element that Paul will develop in his defense speeches at the end of Acts: the promises God made to Israel have found their fulfillment in the resurrection of the Messiah. The whole of Israel's history has been moving, Paul argues, toward Jesus' resurrection from the dead. The resurrection of Jesus, then, is not only God's vindication of Jesus; it is the fulfillment of the promises God made to Israel.

From the point of view of Luke, Paul's sermon in the synagogue of Antioch in Pisidia is an example of the kind of sermon Paul regularly delivered when he spoke to Jews and God-fearers in a synagogue setting. Consequently, instead of reporting other synagogue sermons, Luke provides readers with brief summaries of Paul's preaching intended to remind them of the way in which Paul preached in a Jewish setting. For example, when Paul comes to the synagogue in Thessalonica, Luke writes, "And Paul went in, as was his custom, and on three sabbath days argued with them from the scriptures, explaining and proving *that it was necessary for the Messiah to suffer and to rise from the dead*, and saying, 'This is the Messiah, Jesus whom I am proclaiming to you'" (17:2-3). There is no need for Luke to recount the whole of Paul's preaching at Thessalonica because, having heard the sermon given at Antioch, the readers of Acts now know how Paul preached in a synagogue setting.

### Paul's Witness in Athens

Whereas Paul's synagogue sermon provides us with an example of how he preached to Jews, the speech he delivers in Athens (17:22-31) is an example of how he proclaimed the gospel to Gentiles who were not familiar with the Jewish Scriptures. Faced with such an audience at Athens, Paul must find a new starting point to proclaim the resurrection. This new starting point is the impending judgment of God who created heaven and earth and all who dwell therein.

Paul's speech is occasioned by a request from some Epicurean and Stoic philosophers who are interested in his new teaching about Jesus and the resurrection (17:18). The speech has two parts. In the first, he affirms that he is proclaiming the unknown God whom they worship in ignorance (17:22-28). Then, in the second part, he warns his audience to repent because God is about to judge the world through a man whom he has appointed. Jesus' resurrection, which is the beginning of the general resurrection of the dead, is confirmation of this. In Paul's view, the general resurrection has begun in Jesus, and so the Day of Judgment is at hand (17:29-31).

In the opening of this speech, Paul establishes a relationship with his audience by referring to an altar in Athens dedicated to an unknown God. After praising the Athenians for their piety, he affirms that the God whom they worship unknowingly is the one who made heaven and earth and all that dwell therein. This is the one true God, and they are his offspring.

Having established a relationship with his audience on the basis of their altar dedicated to an unknown God, in the second part of his speech Paul exhorts the Athenians to avoid idolatry and to repent because the Day of Judgment is at hand. Since they are the offspring of God, they should not equate God with any human image or artifact. God has overlooked such idolatrous behavior in the past, but he now requires everyone to repent because "he has fixed a day on which he will have the world judged in righteousness by a man whom he has appointed, and of this he has given assurance to all *by raising him from the dead*" (17:31). While Paul's audience may have agreed with him thus far, his reference to the resurrection of the dead leads some to scoff at him (17:32).

This account of Paul's preaching at Athens has often been viewed as a low point in Paul's career, a moment when he mistakenly sought to preach the gospel on the basis of a natural theology rather than from Scripture. Having made this mistake once, we are told, the apostle never made it again. It seems to me, however, that this is the kind of preaching Paul regularly engaged in when he proclaimed the gospel to Gentiles, as 1 Thessalonians 1:9-10 confirms. Faced with an audience that did not know the story of Israel or the Jewish Scriptures, it was important for Paul to begin his preaching with what his audience could understand. On the basis of this common ground, he then proclaimed the central content of his gospel: *the resurrection of the dead, which has begun in one man, Jesus of Nazareth, and points to the coming judgment of God.*

## Paul's Witness in Jerusalem and Caesarea

In the final part of the Acts of the Apostles, Paul gives a number of speeches in Jerusalem before a Jewish crowd (22:1-21) and the Sanhedrin (23:6), and in Caesarea before the Roman governor Felix

(24:10-21) and the Jewish king Agrippa (26:2-23). These speeches are occasioned by Paul's arrest when a disturbance ensued after he entered the temple with certain Greeks, leading some to accuse him of defiling the temple (21:28). But as the narrative proceeds, it is apparent that the real cause of Paul's imprisonment is his teaching on the resurrection of the dead. Since I have already discussed these speeches in terms of what they tell us about the appearances of the risen Lord (22:1-21; 26:2-23), my remarks in this section are limited to what they tell us about Paul's understanding of the resurrection of the dead.

Paul's defense speech before the crowd in Jerusalem (22:1-21) ends in his arrest and the beginning of his imprisonment. The next day he stands before the Sanhedrin and defends himself by saying, "Brothers, I am a Pharisee, a son of Pharisees. I am on trial concerning the hope of the resurrection of the dead" (23:6). From this point forward, the charge against Paul becomes more and more focused on his teaching about the resurrection of the dead. The real issue according to Paul is the resurrection of the dead, which has begun in the resurrection of Jesus. Thus Paul presents himself as a loyal Pharisaic Jew who has been arrested for preaching the resurrection of the dead. The only difference between him and other Pharisees is that whereas they are still waiting for the resurrection of the dead, Paul proclaims that it has begun in the resurrection of Jesus.

When Paul is transferred to Caesarea, he stands before the Roman governor Felix to defend himself (24:10-21). In his defense, he denies the accusations the Jewish lawyer Tertullus brings against him about creating dissensions among the Jews and desecrating the temple (24:5-6, 12). He affirms that he worships the God of Israel and believes everything written in the Law and the Prophets. He then says, "I have a hope in God—a hope that they themselves also accept—that there will be a resurrection of both the righteous and the unrighteous" (24:15). After affirming his innocence, he concludes that the only crime he has committed, if it can be called a crime, is what he said before the Sanhedrin about his faith in the resurrection of the dead. He concludes, "It is about the resurrection of the dead that I am on trial before you today" (24:21).

The climax of Paul's defense comes in his speech before the Jewish king Agrippa in the presence of the Roman governor Festus (26:2-23). At the outset of his defense, Paul affirms that he is on trial on account of the promises God made to Israel's ancestors, a promise that the twelve tribes of Israel hope to attain (26:6-7). What this promise is becomes apparent in the question Paul asks King Agrippa: "Why is it thought incredible by any of you that God raises the dead?" (26:8). The promise God made to the ancestors, then, is the resurrection of the dead, which has begun in Jesus. After recounting his call and commissioning by the risen Christ, Paul concludes by saying, "To this day I have had help from God, and so I stand here, testifying to both small and great, saying nothing but what the prophets and Moses said would take place: *that the Messiah must suffer, and that, by being the first to rise from the dead*, he would proclaim light both to our people and to the Gentiles" (26:22-23).

By the end of Paul's speeches at Jerusalem and Caesarea, it is clear that from his point of view the issue between him and his fellow Jews is the resurrection of the dead. He believes in the God of Abraham, Isaac, and Jacob and all that is taught in the Law and the Prophets. As a loyal Pharisee, he also believes there will be a general resurrection of the dead. The point of contention is not Paul's loyalty to his ancestral faith but his belief that the hope of Israel—the general resurrection of the dead—has begun in the resurrection of the Messiah.

While Paul's preaching about the resurrection is closely related to Peter's preaching, it develops a theme that Peter's preaching does not: the resurrection of Jesus is the fulfillment of the promise God made to Israel. God's plan for Israel has found its climax in Jesus' resurrection from the dead inasmuch as Jesus' resurrection is the beginning of the general resurrection of the dead.

## The Resurrection in the Acts of the Apostles

The Acts of the Apostles offers a rich harvest for understanding the resurrection of Jesus. The second volume of Luke's two-volume work provides us with insight as to why and how the early church preached the resurrection.

First, the church preached the resurrection because the risen Lord appeared to his apostles over a period of forty days, making them witnesses to his resurrection. By appearing to Paul, the risen one made him a chosen instrument to bear his name to Gentiles, kings, and Israelites. The early church, then, preached the resurrection because the risen one appeared to certain witnesses whom God chose in advance.

Second, the early church preached the resurrection by recounting the story of Jesus within the wider story of Israel. The resurrection is not an aberration of Israel's history; it is the climax of a long history of promise and hope. Confirmation of this can be found in Israel's Scriptures. This means that when the Scriptures are read in light of Jesus' resurrection, it becomes apparent that the promise and hope of Israel is the resurrection of the dead, which has begun in Jesus' resurrection.

The understanding of the resurrection in Acts enriches the understanding of the resurrection we have uncovered in the gospel narratives as it begins to draw out the implications and meaning of the resurrection in ways that point to its significance for Jesus and those who believe in him. The speeches of Acts highlight the christological implications of the resurrection: by raising Jesus, God has enthroned him at his right hand as Lord and Messiah. In addition to enriching our understanding of the risen Lord, these speeches point to the implications of Jesus' resurrection for those who believe in him: their sins are forgiven, they have received the gift of the Spirit, and they will be raised with him. It is these theological implications of the resurrection for the life of believers to which I now turn in our study of the Pauline letters.

# Chapter 4

# The Witness of the Pauline Tradition

In the last chapter I described how, according to the Acts of the Apostles, the early church witnessed to the resurrection. In doing so, I gave special attention to the speeches of Peter and Paul. Although these speeches were given in different circumstances to different audiences, all of them highlight the witness of the early church to the resurrection. The resurrection was not so much a doctrine taught by the early church as it was an experience to which the church witnessed in word and deed because the risen Christ had appeared to chosen witnesses in a compelling way.

Having investigated the witness of Acts, we shall now turn to the witness to the resurrection in the thirteen Pauline letters. Here we will find another powerful witness, perhaps the most powerful testimony to the resurrection in the entire New Testament. But before turning to that testimony, allow me to make a few preliminary remarks.

First, contemporary scholarship distinguishes between seven letters whose Pauline authorship is not disputed (Romans, 1 and 2 Corinthians, Galatians, Philippians, 1 Thessalonians, and Philemon) and six letters whose Pauline authorship is disputed (Ephesians, Colossians, 2 Thessalonians, 1 and 2 Timothy, and Titus). While

I subscribe to this distinction, in this chapter I am approaching the Pauline letters as a body of writings that belongs to the church's canon of Scripture. This means I will deal with all of these letters as Pauline witnesses to the resurrection.

Second, in this chapter I will provide a synthesis of the Pauline witness to the resurrection by organizing my reflections around the following topics: Paul's encounter with the risen Christ, the traditions Paul received from the early church about the resurrection, the resurrection of the body, the Spirit and the resurrection, the resurrection and the church, the resurrection life of the justified, the resurrection and the renewal of creation. In choosing these topics, I am not claiming that all of them appear with the same force in each of the Pauline letters. They do not. Moreover, readers will soon notice that Romans and the Corinthian correspondence receive more attention than other letters. By approaching the material in this way, however, I seek to present readers with a helpful overview of the Pauline material.

Third, while I am approaching the Pauline writings as a collection of letters, I am keenly aware that all of the letters (whether written by Paul or not) were composed in response to particular circumstances rather than as theological essays. Accordingly, I respect what is often called the "occasional nature" of the Pauline letters: the fact that the composition of each of them was occasioned by particular historical circumstances.

Any attempt to synthesize in one chapter what the Pauline letters witness to the resurrection is doomed to failure. The reality of the resurrection so suffuses these letters that there is hardly a chapter that does not, in some way, witness to the resurrection. For example, consider the titles these letters employ: Lord, Christ, Son, Son of God, Savior. All of them are applied to Jesus in virtue of the resurrection. Or, consider these simple phrases that occur again and again in these letters: "in Christ," "with Christ," "through Christ." Each of them points to a union with Christ made possible by the resurrection. Or, consider what these letters say about the Spirit or the church, all of which presupposes the resurrection of Christ. In a word, the resurrection is that without which there would be no

Pauline theology. Everything these letters say, all that Paul writes and witnesses to, presupposes that God raised Jesus from the dead. If God did not raise Jesus from the dead, our faith is in vain and we are still in our sins (1 Cor 15:17). And so, although synthesizing the Pauline witness to the resurrection is like trying to contain the ocean in a bucket, I hope this chapter will provide readers with a starting point for understanding the Pauline witness to the resurrection.

## Paul's Encounter with the Risen Christ

Any discussion of the resurrection in the Pauline tradition should begin with Paul's call to be the apostle to the Gentiles. It was at that moment that Paul, who was so zealous for the Mosaic Law that he persecuted and tried to destroy the church, encountered the risen Lord. At that moment, God revealed his Son to him, and Paul understood that the crucified Jesus whom he viewed as under God's curse (Gal 3:13) was none other than God's Son, the Messiah. From that point forward it became necessary for Paul to rethink his understanding of the law of Moses and Israel's covenant relationship to God in terms of Christ. Whereas Paul once viewed Christ from a merely human point of view, that is to say, according to the flesh, after his call and conversion he could no longer evaluate Christ in that way (2 Cor 5:16). For the same God, who at the creation of the world said, "Let light shine out of darkness," revealed to Paul "the light of the knowledge of the glory of God in the face of Jesus Christ" (2 Cor 4:6). Accordingly, Paul now began to understand that the crucified Jesus was not a lawbreaker under God's curse, as he once thought. Rather, the one whom God raised from the dead was "the end of the Law," that is to say, the goal and purpose of the Mosaic Law (Rom 10:4). To know the risen Christ, then, is to know "the mystery of God" (1 Cor 2:1), "a plan for the fullness of time, to gather up all things in him, things in heaven and things on earth" (Eph 1:10).

The central text in which Paul refers to his call occurs in Galatians, a harsh polemical letter in which Paul must defend (1) his right to be called an apostle and (2) the gospel he preaches among the Gentiles: that one is justified on the basis of faith in Christ rather than on the basis of doing the works of the Mosaic Law (Gal 2:16). Paul's account of his call is part of an extended autobiographical statement in Galatians 1–2, in which the apostle points to certain events of his life to assure the Galatians that his call to be an apostle and the gospel he preached to them is not of human origin but comes from "a revelation of Jesus Christ" (Gal 1:12).

Paul's account begins with a brief statement of his former way of life (Gal 1:13-14). Before he was called to be an apostle, he persecuted the church of God with the intent of utterly destroying it. Deeply rooted in the traditions of his Jewish ancestors, Paul claims that he was more zealous for these traditions (whose purpose was to preserve and guard the Law) than any of his contemporaries. Paul leaves us with the impression that his zeal for the Law bordered on fanaticism.

It is after describing his former way of life that Paul turns to his call: "But *when God, who had set me apart before I was born and called me through his grace, was pleased to reveal his Son to me, so that I might proclaim him among the Gentiles,* I did not confer with any human being, nor did I go up to Jerusalem to those who were already apostles before me, but I went away at once into Arabia, and afterwards I returned to Damascus" (Gal 1:15-17). Paul's account of his call is brief and sparse. It is not told as part of an extended narrative such as we find in Acts 9, 22, and 26. There is no description of the risen Christ. Paul simply says God revealed his Son to him. But there are other texts in Paul's letters that suggest something more than a mere subjective experience. For example, in 1 Corinthians 9:1 he asserts his right to be called an apostle: "Am I not free? Am I not an apostle? *Have I not seen Jesus our Lord?* Are you not my work in the Lord?" Similarly, in 1 Corinthians 15:8, after listing those to whom the risen Christ appeared, he writes, "Last of all, as to one untimely born, *he appeared also to me.*"

Paul's discussion about his apostolic ministry in 2 Corinthians provides us with some insight into how the risen Christ appeared to him. Comparing his ministry with the ministry of Moses, Paul insists that as glorious as the ministry of Moses was, his own ministry is more glorious because it enables believers to gaze on the glory of the Lord and be "transformed into the same image from one degree of glory to another" (2 Cor 3:18). The "image" to which Paul refers here is the image of the risen Christ who is the image of God on whose face shines the glory of God (2 Cor 4:4, 6). What Paul saw, then, was the glory of the risen Christ who is now the image of God, the one who will conform Paul's lowly body to his own glorified body (Phil 3:21). This is why Luke describes Paul's encounter with the risen Lord in terms of "a light from heaven," "a great light from heaven," "a light from heaven, brighter than the sun" (Acts 9:3; 22:6; 26:13). By portraying Paul's encounter with the risen Lord in this way, Luke suggests that Paul encountered the risen Lord in his resurrection glory. When Paul says that God revealed his Son to him, or when he writes that he has seen the Lord, he means he has seen the glory of the risen Christ who now shares in the very glory of God.

Paul's encounter with the risen Lord defined his ministry, and it was in light of this encounter that he exercised his ministry. This is why many of his letters begin with an allusion to his call. For example, "Paul, a servant of Jesus Christ, *called* to be an apostle" (Rom 1:1); "Paul, *called* to be an apostle of Christ" (1 Cor 1:1); "Paul, an apostle of Christ Jesus *by the will of God*" (Col 1:1); "Paul, an apostle of Christ Jesus *by the will of God*, for the sake of the promise of life that is in Christ Jesus" (2 Tim 1:1). While Paul certainly learned from the traditions of the church, and while his ministry gave him an ever deeper insight into the gospel he preached, it was the foundational experience of his call, when God revealed his Son to him, that determined Paul's understanding of the gospel he preached, especially his witness to the resurrection.

## Creedal Statements, Summaries of the Faith, Hymns

In addition to his encounter with the risen Lord, Paul inherited traditions about the resurrection, and he contributed to the growth of this tradition by adding his own summaries of the faith he proclaimed. Apart from those instances when he explicitly says that he inherited such traditions (1 Cor 11:23; 15:3), however, it is difficult to say with certainty if a particular tradition comes from Paul or from the church. Accordingly, without entering into the technical question of whether or not Paul received or created such traditions, I will point to and discuss a series of creedal statements, summaries of the faith, and hymns that provide us with further insight into the Pauline understanding of the resurrection.

The most important of these traditions is 1 Corinthians 15:3-5, which occurs at the beginning of a chapter in which Paul must defend the bodily nature of the resurrection and explain what he means by the resurrection body. Before undertaking this task, however, Paul reminds the Corinthians of the essential content of the gospel he preached to them. To do this, he recalls a tradition he received and handed on to them:

> For I handed on to you as of first importance what I in turn had received: that Christ *died* for our sins in accordance with the scriptures, and that he was *buried*, and that he was *raised* on the third day in accordance with the scriptures, and that he *appeared* to Cephas, then to the twelve.

The manner in which I have emphasized this text highlights two things. First, Paul says that Jesus *died*, that he was *buried*, that he was *raised*, and that he *appeared* to Cephas (Peter) and the Twelve. While the two essential moments in Christ's redemptive work are his death and resurrection, it is his burial that confirms that he truly died, and it is his appearance to Peter that confirms that God raised him from the dead. Second, the phrase "in accordance with the scriptures," which occurs twice, shows that the death of Christ was not just a miscarriage of justice since his death and resurrection were foreseen in Israel's Scriptures. Accordingly, while brief, this tradition that Paul received and handed on to the Corinthians summarizes the essential content of his gospel, that without which there is no gospel, namely, faith in the death and resurrection of Jesus Christ.

After these verses, Paul lists other persons to whom the risen Lord appeared: five hundred others in one appearance, James, all the apostles (a group that Paul views as larger than the Twelve), and last of all Paul himself (1 Cor 15:6-9). Whether or not these other appearances (apart from the appearance to Paul) were part of the tradition he received is difficult to say. But even if they were not, they strengthen the earliest tradition by showing how well-attested the resurrection is.

In 1 Thessalonians Paul provides us with two texts that give us an insight into how he preached among his earliest converts. Like the text from 1 Corinthians 15, they may reflect earlier traditions that Paul received or, more likely, they show us how he was beginning to summarize his own understanding of the faith. For example, the text of 1 Thessalonians 1:9-10 summarizes Paul's preaching to the Thessalonians:

> For the people of those regions report about us what kind of welcome we had among you, and how you turned to God from idols, to serve a living and true God, and to wait for his Son from heaven, *whom he raised from the dead*—Jesus, who rescues us from the wrath that is coming.

When he came to Thessalonica, Paul exhorted the Thessalonians to turn from idols and serve the living and true God, the God of Israel. Paul makes this exhortation because the Day of Judgment is at hand inasmuch as the resurrection of the dead has begun in Jesus, God's Son. If the Thessalonians hope to be rescued by Jesus on the day of God's judgment, they must believe in the one God. In this text, then, the resurrection of Jesus signals that the end of the ages has come.

In 1 Thessalonians 4:14 Paul provides something akin to a creedal formula or summary of the faith to assure the Thessalonians that the members of their community who have died will be rescued by Jesus when he returns, even though they have died: "For since *we believe that Jesus died and rose again*, even so, through Jesus, God will bring with him those who have died." The essential content of the Christian faith, as we have already seen from 1 Corinthians 15:3-5, is the death and resurrection of Jesus Christ. Those who believe in this can be assured they will participate in God's salvation, even if they die before the Parousia, since the resurrection of Christ is not an isolated event that only touches him. The resurrection of Christ is the beginning of the general resurrection from the dead.

Paul's great letter to the Romans contains several texts that may have been earlier creedal statements or summaries of the faith Paul inherited, edited, or even created to summarize the essential content of the gospel he proclaims. The first of these texts occurs at the outset of the letter and is usually viewed as a tradition Paul inherited:

> [T]he gospel concerning his Son, who was descended from David *according to the flesh* and was declared to be Son of God with power *according to the spirit of holiness* by resurrection from the dead, Jesus Christ our Lord. (Rom 1:3-4)

Here we find a contrast between two phases in Christ's life. The first is his earthly origin and descent from David, which qualified him to be the Messiah. The second is the resurrection, when he was established in power as the messianic Son of God. Whereas his earthly descent was according to the flesh, his enthronement as God's messianic Son was a powerful act of God's Spirit, whereby God raised him from the dead. Jesus' status as the messianic Son of God cannot be understood apart from the resurrection, and his resurrection cannot be understood apart from God's Spirit.

Another creedal-like statement occurs in Romans 4 at the end of Paul's exposition of Abraham's faith, which he likens to resurrection faith because Abraham believed in God "*who gives life to the dead and calls into existence the things that do not exist*" (4:17). At the end of his discussion of Abraham's faith, Paul concludes,

> Now the words, "it was reckoned to him," were written not for his sake alone, but for ours also. It will be reckoned to us *who believe in him who raised Jesus our Lord from the dead, who was handed over to death for our trespasses and was raised for our justification.* (Rom 4:23-25)

Here, Paul applies what he has said about Abraham to those who believe in Christ: just as Abraham was justified because he believed in God's promises, so will those who believe in God who raised

Jesus from the dead be justified. Paul then describes God's work in Christ in two ways: first, Christ was handed over for our transgressions; second, he was raised for our justification. This creedal-like statement has always been problematic since it seems to assign the forgiveness of sins to Christ's death and justification to his resurrection, as if Christ's death had nothing to do with justification and his resurrection had nothing to do with the forgiveness of sins. God's redemptive work in Christ, however, is a single event that includes Christ's death and resurrection. Thus it is Christ's death and resurrection that effects the remission of sins and his death and resurrection that justifies the sinner. In assigning specific tasks to Christ's death and resurrection, Paul provides believers with a way to remember what is central to their faith.

Another brief summary of the faith that Paul proclaims appears at the end of Romans 8, a chapter in which Paul discusses the role of the Spirit in the Christian life. Paul ends that chapter with a rhetorical flourish to assure the justified that nothing can separate them from God's love for them:

> Who is to condemn? It is Christ Jesus, who died, yes, who was raised, who is at the right hand of God, who indeed intercedes for us. (Rom 8:34)

This statement reveals the full scope of God's redemptive work in Christ: death, resurrection, exaltation, and intercession. Like Romans 4:25, this text highlights different phases in a single redemptive event. Believers can be confident they will not be condemned because God's redemptive work, which begins with Christ's death and concludes with his resurrection and exaltation, makes Christ their intercessor before God.

In addition to these summaries and creedal-like formulas, the Pauline letters contain a number of hymn-like passages in which the resurrection of Christ or the believer plays a central role. The best known of these are Philippians 2:5-11 and Colossians 1:15-20.

The Philippians hymn describes the "career" of Christ as a movement from self-abasement (2:6-8) to exaltation (2:9-11). Although Christ was "in the form of God," he humbled himself to the point of dying on the cross. Because of this, God "highly exalted him." In this hymn, the resurrection is portrayed as God's vindication of Jesus, the moment when God exalted him by bestowing upon him the divine name, "Lord."

The Colossians hymn also has a two-part structure. In the first part (1:15-17), the hymn celebrates Christ as "the firstborn of all creation," the one through whom and for whom God created all things. In the second part (1:18-20), Christ is called "the firstborn from the dead," the one through whom and for whom all things were reconciled to God. The phrase, "the firstborn from the dead," points to Christ's resurrection, which is the beginning of the general resurrection from the dead.

Although these two hymns are different (the Philippians hymn highlighting the career of Christ, and the Colossians hymn celebrating his role in creation and redemption), both point to the cosmic scope of Christ's resurrection. By the resurrection God exalted Jesus and gave him his own name ("Lord") so that every tongue must acclaim him as "Lord," and he made him the firstborn from the dead, the one who is revealed as the agent and goal of God's creative and redemptive work.

In addition to these hymns, there are three shorter hymn-like passages that highlight the importance of the resurrection. The first is a baptismal hymn that draws out the implications of Christ's resurrection for the newly baptized. Previous to their baptism, they were dead, living in the darkness of sin. Now that they have been raised to new life in Christ, they live in the light of God's life: "Sleeper, awake! / *Rise from the dead*, / and Christ will shine on you" (Eph 5:14).

The second provides a summary of what 1 Timothy calls "the mystery of our religion" (3:16). The hymn summarizes the "career" of Christ: He appeared in the flesh (the incarnation); he was vindicated in the Spirit (the resurrection); angels saw the risen one; the resurrection was proclaimed among the Gentiles and believed in throughout the world. Finally, he was taken up into heaven (the ascension). Here, everything hinges on the resurrection: Jesus' vindication by the Spirit of God:

He was revealed in flesh,
  *vindicated in spirit,*
    seen by angels,
proclaimed among Gentiles,
  believed in throughout the world,
    taken up in glory.

The third passage is presented as a reliable saying that believers can depend upon (2 Tim 2:11-12). It assures them that if they adopt the pattern of Christ's suffering and death in their lives, they will participate in Christ's resurrection life:

If we have died with him, *we will also live with him*;
if we endure, *we will also reign with him*;
if we deny him, he will also deny us.

Hymns, unlike dogmatic formulas, appeal to our imagination. They help us to celebrate what we believe and express it in new, imaginative ways. In some of these hymns the resurrection is portrayed as cosmic in scope, something that affects the whole of creation as well as the individual. In others, the resurrection provides believers with a paradigm for their lives: if they follow the pattern of Christ's life in their life, God will vindicate them as he vindicated Christ.

## The Resurrection of the Body

Paul steadfastly believed in the bodily resurrection of Jesus and of those who believe in him. The resurrection is not just a metaphor for eternal life. Nor does it merely refer to a spiritual rising to new life in Christ. The body plays an essential role in Paul's theology of the resurrection: the body of Christ has been raised and the bodies of those who believe in him will be raised. We have already seen that the evangelists witness to the bodily resurrection of Jesus and, by implication, the bodily resurrection of those who believe in him. But no other writer presents us with such a sophisticated understanding of the bodily resurrection of Christ and of those who believe in him as does Paul. In his letters, especially in his Corinthian correspondence, he wrestles with the concept of the resurrection body. What he writes about the resurrection body gives us further insight into his understanding of the risen Christ.

Paul takes up the question of the resurrection in 1 Corinthians 15, a chapter in which he must answer two questions: Will there be a bodily resurrection? If so, what is the resurrection body like? These questions arise because the Corinthians have misunderstood the gospel he proclaimed to them. Although they believe in Christ's death and resurrection and have some understanding of its meaning for their lives, they have a merely spiritual understanding of Christ's resurrection and their participation in it. Yes, they affirm God raised Christ to new life. Yes, they will be raised to new life in Christ, a life they have begun to experience in the Spirit. But they do not see the need for a bodily resurrection. After all, is not the body the tomb from which Christ has freed them? Is it not the body that holds them back from union with God?

In the face of this misunderstanding, Paul reminds the Corinthians of the tradition about Christ's death and resurrection that he received and handed on to them: Christ died, he was buried, he was raised on the third day, and he appeared in bodily form to a host of witnesses, many of whom are still alive (15:1-11).

After reminding the Corinthians of the gospel of Christ's death and resurrection that the church preaches, Paul argues that if there is no resurrection of the dead, then Christ has not been raised from the dead—for, Christ's resurrection was the beginning of the long-awaited general resurrection of the dead (15:12-28). Christ's resurrection, Paul argues, was not an isolated event but the beginning of a new creation, the beginning of the general resurrection of the dead. To deny that the dead are raised is to deny that Christ has been raised from the dead since the risen Christ is the "first fruits" of the general resurrection of the dead (15:23).

To this point in his argument, Paul has presupposed the bodily resurrection of Christ and of those who believe in him. In the final part of his argument (1 Cor 15:35-58), however, he addresses the question head on: "But someone will ask, 'How are the dead raised? With what kind of body do they come?'" (v. 35). To answer this question, Paul uses three examples from everyday life. The plant that grows from the seed buried in the ground is in continuity and yet different from the seed (15:36-38). The flesh of human beings and animals is similar to but different from each other (15:39). There are different kinds of celestial bodies and each has a different brightness (15:40-41). And so it is with the earthly and the resurrection body. The earthly body is perishable, dishonorable and weak, but when it is raised as a resurrection body it is imperishable, glorious, and powerful (15:42-43). The earthly body is physical; the resurrection body is spiritual (15:44).

But what does Paul mean by a spiritual body? Is he, after all, adopting the same view of the resurrection as the Corinthians? Not at all!

In the next section (15:45-49), Paul draws a contrast between the first Adam and the New or eschatological Adam, who is Christ. The first Adam, the man of sin, was a "living being" because he was animated by the natural life principle called the soul. The second Adam, the New Man, the eschatological man, was a "life-giving spirit" because he is animated by God's own Spirit (15:45). Both men, the first and the New Adam, are embodied beings; both have bodies. But whereas the body of the first was made alive by the ordinary life principle, the body of the second is animated by God's own Spirit. This is why Paul speaks of a "spiritual body." Such a body is real and corporeal but in an entirely new way since it has been changed and transformed by God's Spirit. It is no longer bound by the limitations of time and space. It will always live without change and corruption because it has been given God's own life through the power of God's Spirit.

Making use of this Adam-Christ comparison, Paul affirms that whereas in our earthly existence we bear the image of the first Adam, at the resurrection we will bear the image of the eschatological Adam; that is, we will become like the risen Lord whose body has been transformed by God's Spirit. This is why Paul writes, "But our citizenship is in heaven, and it is from there that we are expecting a Savior, the Lord Jesus Christ. He will transform the body of our humiliation *that it may be conformed to the body of his glory,* by the power that also enables him to make all things subject to himself" (Phil 3:20-21). The bodies of those who believe in Christ will be conformed to the body of the risen Christ, a body Paul describes as glorious because it has been transformed by God's Spirit and so reflects God's glory.

Paul concludes his discussion of the resurrection body with a description of what will happen at the general resurrection of the dead (15:50-57). He begins by insisting that the body we now inhabit, a body of flesh and blood, cannot enter the kingdom of God—the sphere of God's own being. To enter God's kingdom one must be changed and transformed. This process, Paul says, will be instantaneous. The bodies of those who have not died before the general resurrection as well as of those who have died will be changed and forever transformed by the power of God's Spirit. The earthly body, which is perishable and mortal, will be clothed with imperishability and immortality, that is, with a resurrection body that is a spiritual body because it has been transformed by God's Spirit.

Paul takes up the topic of the resurrection body from a different vantage point in 2 Corinthians 5:1-10 when he employs the metaphors of a "tent" and a "building" to describe the present body of the believer and the resurrection body the believer will inherit. The bodies of those who believe in Christ are as fragile as an earthly tent that is liable to collapse at any moment. Paul, however, is not disheartened because he is confident that if this tent—his earthly body—collapses, God will provide him with a resurrection body that Paul portrays as "a building from God, a house not made with hands, eternal in the heavens" (5:1). Although the imagery Paul employs here does not highlight the continuity between the earthly body and the resurrection body in the way that 1 Corinthians 15 does, it makes the same point about the bodily resurrection. Those who rise in Christ will rise with a body, albeit a body that has been changed and transformed. That body, as 2 Corinthians shows, cannot be shaken or destroyed because it is an eternal building made by God rather than by human beings.

## The Spirit and the Resurrection

Paul's discussion about the resurrection body highlights the role that the Spirit of God plays in the resurrection of Christ and of those who believe in him. The resurrection body is a "spiritual body" because it is a transformed body animated by the very Spirit of God. It is a body whose life-principle is no longer the soul but God's Spirit. Accordingly, the resurrection body is no longer subject to change or decay. Like the resurrection body of the New Man, Jesus Christ, it is eternally young because it is eternally new.[1]

Paul's most extensive discussion of the relationship between the Spirit and the resurrection of the dead occurs in Romans 8. In that chapter, he describes the new situation in which the justified find themselves in light of Christ's saving death and resurrection. They no longer belong to the realm of the flesh, which is mortal and destined for corruption, but to the realm of the Spirit, which is immortal and incorruptible because the Spirit of God dwells in them (8:9). Paul then affirms that the presence of this Spirit within the justified assures them that they will share in Christ's resurrection:

> If the Spirit *of him who raised Jesus from the dead* dwells in you, *he who raised Christ from the dead* will give life to your mortal bodies also through his Spirit that dwells in you. (Rom 8:11)

We must read this text carefully. Paul does not say that the Spirit raised Jesus from the dead. He writes that the Spirit *of him*, namely, God the Father, who raised Jesus from the dead. He then goes on to say that God will also raise from the dead, *through the power of his Spirit*, those in whom his Spirit dwells. It is God who raises the dead through the power of his Spirit.

Next, Paul draws a relationship between the Spirit and the adoption of the justified as God's children (8:14-17). Those who are led by the Spirit are God's children because they have received a spirit of adoption that empowers them to call God "Abba! Father!" just as Jesus did. Having become God's adopted sons and daughters through the power of the Spirit, they have become "joint heirs with Christ" if they suffer with Christ. For if they suffer with him, they will be "glorified with him"; they will be raised from the dead.

The Spirit's presence in the life of the justified is the assurance of their resurrection from the dead; it is the first taste of the resurrection life that those who believe in Christ already experience. Paul writes that the justified, who have "the first fruits of the Spirit," groan with the whole of creation because they are waiting for "the redemption" of their bodies that will occur at the general resurrection of the dead (Rom 8:23). He calls the Spirit "a first installment" (2 Cor 1:22), "the pledge of our inheritance" (Eph 1:14), and "a seal" with which believers are marked "for the day of redemption" (Eph 4:30). Although the vocabulary differs, each of these texts makes a similar point: The Spirit is the assurance of resurrection from the dead. Like the first installment one pays to guarantee the delivery of goods purchased, the Spirit is God's pledge and seal that designates the justified as destined for resurrection life.

Paul's letter to Titus draws another connection between the gift of the Spirit and the resurrection of the dead without explicitly mentioning the resurrection of the dead:

> But when the goodness and loving kindness of God our Savior appeared, he saved us, not because of any works of righteousness that we had done, but according to his mercy, *through the water of rebirth and renewal by the Holy Spirit. This Spirit he poured out on us richly through Jesus Christ our Savior, so that, having been justified by his grace, we might become heirs according to the hope of eternal life.* (Titus 3:4-7)

Here the focus is on the effects of baptism, "the water of rebirth." Baptism is the moment when the Spirit, like water, was poured upon believers and justified them by God's grace. By justifying them by God's grace, the Spirit has made them "heirs" to the hope of eternal life, which is the resurrection from the dead.

To sum up, it is the presence and experience of the Spirit, the powerful Spirit by which God raised Jesus from the dead, that assures believers that God will raise them from the dead just as he raised Jesus from the dead—for, the same Spirit that believers now experience will change and transform them on the day of resurrection just as it changed and transformed the crucified Jesus.

## The Resurrection and the Church

Paul views the community of believers to whom he writes as "the church," or "the church of God," a sanctified assembly called into being by God's redemptive work in Christ's death and resurrection. Accordingly, the church is not merely a gathering of like-minded believers who have decided to live in fellowship with one another. It is an assembly of those elected and called into being by God. This is why Paul employs the language of call and election when he writes to the churches. For example, he begins his first letter to the Corinthians, "To the church of God that is in Corinth, to those who are *sanctified* in Christ Jesus, *called* to be saints, together with all those who in every place call on the name of our Lord Jesus Christ, both their Lord and ours" (1 Cor 1:2). In the great benediction that opens the letter to the Ephesians, he writes, "In Christ we have also obtained an inheritance, having been *destined* according to the purpose of him who accomplishes all things according to his counsel and will" (Eph 1:11). For Paul the church is an assembly of the elect whom God has sanctified and called into existence through Christ. This assembly of the elect came into existence through Christ's death and resurrection.

Although we often think of the death and resurrection of Christ as two distinct acts, one that happened on Good Friday and the other on Easter Sunday, the death and resurrection of Christ form a single redemptive act. Accordingly, while we speak of Christ's atoning death on the cross and the new life that comes from his resurrection, the atonement is the result of Christ's resurrection as well as his death, and the new life believers enjoy in Christ is the result of Christ's death as well as his resurrection. God's redemptive work in Christ is a single act of redemption that consists of Christ's death *and* resurrection.

When we acknowledge the unity of God's redemptive work in Christ, it becomes clear that *the church comes into existence through this redemptive act.* By putting forth Christ as "a sacrifice of atonement" (Rom 3:25) and declaring him to be "Son of God with power according to the spirit of holiness by resurrection from the dead" (Rom 1:4), God called the church into existence "not from the Jews only but also from the Gentiles" (Rom 9:24). Any theology of the church, then, must take into account the central role of God's redemptive work in Christ.

In addition to speaking of the assembly of those who believe in Christ as "the church," Paul also calls them the temple of God and the body of Christ. Believers have become the new, that is, the eschatological temple of God because the Spirit of God released by Christ's death and resurrection dwells in their midst. And so Paul writes, "Do you not know that *you are God's temple and that God's Spirit dwells in you*? If anyone destroys God's temple, God will destroy that person. For God's temple is holy, *and you are that temple*" (1 Cor 3:16-17). Whereas Paul formerly viewed the temple of Jerusalem as the locus of God's presence, he now views his Gentile converts as the temple of God's presence, not because of their personal holiness but because God's Spirit dwells in their midst. In Ephesians, a letter whose Pauline authorship is disputed, a similar point is made in a more developed manner. Writing to Gentiles, the apostle affirms,

> So then you are no longer strangers and aliens, but you are citizens with the saints and also members of the household of God, built upon the foundation of the apostles and prophets, with Christ Jesus himself as the cornerstone. *In him the whole structure is joined together and grows into a holy temple in the Lord; in whom you also are built together spiritually into a dwelling place for God.* (Eph 2:19-22)

What Paul writes here presupposes the saving event of Christ's death and resurrection. Christ is the "cornerstone" of this structure because he is the stone the builders rejected but which God has chosen by raising him from the dead. This Lord to whom believers have been joined is the crucified and risen Lord. Apart from his death and resurrection there is no church; there is no eschatological temple.

Paul's most important description of the church is as the body of Christ. Given the complexity of this metaphor, I will limit my discussion to the following texts:

> Now *you are the body of Christ* and individually members of it. (1 Cor 12:27)

> For as in one body we have many members, and not all the members have the same function, *so we, who are many, are one body in Christ*, and individually we are members one of another. (Rom 12:4-5)

*He is the head of the body, the church*; he is the beginning, the firstborn from the dead, so that he might come to have first place in everything. (Col 1:18)

*And he has put all things under his feet and has made him the head over all things for the church, which is his body*, the fullness of him who fills all in all. (Eph 1:22-23)

But speaking the truth in love, *we must grow up in every way into him who is the head, into Christ, from whom the whole body, joined and knit together by every ligament with which it is equipped*, as each part is working properly, promotes the body's growth in building itself up in love. (Eph 4:15-16)

In all of these texts Paul draws a relationship between the community of those who believe in Christ and the body of Christ. But what body? Given what he writes in these texts, it is apparent that Paul is not just speaking of the body of the earthly Jesus. He is referring to the crucified body that was transformed into the resurrection body of the crucified and risen Christ. Paul has in view the resurrection body of Christ that will forever remain in continuity with his crucified body. Because the resurrection body of Christ is not limited by the confines of time and space, believers can live in this crucified and risen body. And because they have the Spirit of God, which is the Spirit of Christ (see Rom 8:9), believers form the body of Christ. This is why the church, which is the body of Christ, comes into being at the death and resurrection of Christ. For at that moment the crucified and risen Lord communicates the Spirit of God with which he is filled to those who believe in him, thereby making them the temple of God and members of his glorified body.

The Pauline letters present this understanding of the church as the body of Christ in two ways. In 1 Corinthians and Romans the metaphor takes on a more functional role. Each member of the Christian community by virtue of being baptized into the crucified and risen body of Christ has become one Spirit with Christ (1 Cor 6:17). Having been baptized into Christ, each member now plays a distinctive role in the body of Christ according to the particular gift of the Spirit that he or she has received. Thus the church is a body with each member functioning in a different way for the good of the whole body. This is why Paul says that believers are the body of Christ (1 Cor 12:27), each member forming one body in Christ (Rom 12:5).

Colossians and Ephesians employ the body metaphor in a slightly different way, distinguishing between the head and the body rather than focusing on the different functions of the members of the body. The head of the body is the crucified and risen Lord who is "the firstborn from the dead" (Col 1:18), and it is into the head of the body that the church must grow. This use of the metaphor of the church as the body joined to Christ the head emphasizes that the body must grow into the head.

Because the church is related to the risen Lord as a body is to its head, Paul writes, "when you were buried with him in baptism, *you were also raised with him through faith in the power of God*, who raised him from the dead" (Col 2:12). Ephesians goes further: "But God, who is rich in mercy, out of the great love with which he loved us even when we were dead through our trespasses, made us alive together with Christ—by grace you have been saved—*and raised us up with him and seated us with him in the heavenly places in Christ Jesus*" (Eph 2:4-6). Because the church is the body of Christ, Paul predicates of the church what he predicates of Christ—for if the head has been raised up and seated in the heavenly places, the body is present there as well. There is a sense, then, in which believers are already raised up and enthroned with Christ.

To conclude, although Paul never explicitly says that the church was created by Christ's saving death and resurrection, what he writes about the church justifies this statement. For, inasmuch as the church is the assembly of those elected in light of Christ's death and resurrection, the temple of God's Spirit, and the body of the crucified and risen Lord, it was born through Christ's death and resurrection.

## The Resurrection and the Life of the Justified

The resurrection not only transformed the life of the crucified Jesus; it also transforms the life of those who are justified in God's presence through faith in Christ. Consequently, although the justified are still waiting for the day when their bodies will be conformed to the body of the risen Christ, the firstborn from the dead, they are already experiencing the newness of life that comes from the power of the Spirit released by Christ's resurrection. Justified by God's redemptive work in Christ and saved by God's grace, they no longer live in the realm of the flesh that characterizes life in Adam but in the realm of the Spirit that characterizes life in the eschatological Adam, the New Man, who is Jesus Christ. The justified live in the community of the church, which is the body of the crucified and risen Christ. This new situation means that they already experience something of their Lord's resurrection life through the gift of the Spirit. Because they do, they can and ought to live in the newness of life that the Spirit of God makes possible.

The justified were first conformed to Christ by their baptism into his death and resurrection. This baptism was more than a ritual bath; it was a moment of profound faith in the crucified and risen Christ when they sacramentally participated in the event that is the object of their faith: Christ's death and resurrection. Paul refers to the power of this moment:

> What then are we to say? Should we continue in sin in order that grace may abound? By no means! How can we who died to sin go on living in it? Do you not know that all of us who have been baptized into Christ Jesus were baptized into his death? Therefore we have been buried with him by baptism into death, so that, *just as Christ was raised from the dead by the glory of the Father, so we too might walk in newness of life.* (Rom 6:1-4)

Paul reminds the Romans of the significance of their baptismal union with Christ in order to dissuade them from thinking that God's abundant grace does away with the need to live a morally good life. Sin should no longer play a role in the life of the justified because it no longer has the power over their lives that it had when they lived in the old Adam. By their baptismal union with Christ, they share in Christ's victory over the power of sin: they died and were buried with him so that just as Christ was raised from the dead, they might be raised to "newness of life," by which Paul means life in the Spirit of their risen Lord.

Paul is ever mindful that the resurrection of the justified is yet to occur. But there is a condition for participation in Christ's resurrection: if the justified hope to share in the resurrection, they must share in their Lord's suffering and death. This relationship between participation in Christ's death and resurrection is evident in the following texts:

> For if we have been united with him in a death like his, we will certainly be united with him in a resurrection like his. (Rom 6:5)

> But if we have died with Christ, we believe that we will also live with him. (Rom 6:8)

Just as Christ's resurrection could not occur until after his passion and death, so the resurrection of those who believe in him requires that they pass through a similar passion and death if they hope to attain the fullness of the resurrection life, which at the present time they experience in an anticipatory way through their life in the Spirit.

It is this life in the Spirit, which is a foretaste of the fullness of resurrection life, that empowers the justified to live a morally good life. One lives either in the realm of the flesh, the old Adam, or in the realm of the Spirit, the New Adam. Those who live "in the flesh cannot please God" (Rom 8:8) because they do not have the inner power of the Spirit to fulfill God's law as they ought. Those who live in the realm of the Spirit, however, have been empowered to live in a new way that accords with God's will. Whereas those who live in the old Adam continue to produce "the works of the flesh" (Gal 5:19), the Spirit of the risen Lord produces its fruit in those who live in the realm of the Spirit: "love, joy, peace, patience, kindness, generosity, faithfulness, gentleness, and self-control" (Gal 5:22-23).

The newness of life in which the justified live is a life in union with Christ whereby they participate in his death and resurrection, and it is their participation in this pattern of death and life that now determines their moral life.

In Colossians and Ephesians, we detect a shift in the way Paul or those writing in his name portray the believer's present experience of the resurrection. Because of the distinctive way in which they describe the church as the body of Christ, Colossians and Ephesians emphasize, in a way that Romans does not, the present experience of the resurrection the justified enjoy. Several texts are pertinent here:

> [W]hen you were buried with him in baptism, *you were also raised with him through faith in the power of God, who raised him from the dead.* And when you were dead in trespasses and the uncircumcision of your flesh, God made you alive together with him, when he forgave us all our trespasses. (Col 2:12-13)

Like Romans 6, this text affirms that the believer was buried with Christ in baptism, but unlike Romans it proclaims that the believer has been raised up with Christ "through faith in the power of God, who raised [Christ] from the dead." Colossians, of course, knows that the bodily resurrection of the believer has not yet occurred, as is evident from the phrase "raised with him through faith." But given its understanding of the church as the body and Christ as the head of the body, it affirms that there is a sense in which the believer is already raised up since the head of the body to which the believer belongs has been raised up.

A similar text occurs in Colossians 3 but this time with mention of moral implications for those who are associated with Christ's resurrection:

> So if you have been raised with Christ, seek the things that are above, where Christ is, seated at the right hand of God. Set your minds on things that are above, not on things that are on earth, for you have died, and your life is hidden with Christ in God. When Christ who is your life is revealed, then you also will be revealed with him in glory. (Col 3:1-4)

Colossians does not have a naïve understanding of the resurrection, as if it had already occurred, since it affirms that the resurrection life of the believer will only be revealed at the general resurrection of the dead when Christ returns. What Colossians says is that inasmuch as believers belong to the body of Christ they have been raised up with their head. Consequently, they should pursue those things that pertain to heaven, where Christ is enthroned. It is no coincidence that after this opening statement, Paul calls the Colossians to live a morally good life, exhorting them to "put to death" what is earthly (Col 3:5) and clothe themselves "with the new self, which is being renewed in knowledge according to the image of its creator" (Col 3:10). This "new self" is the new humanity created by their Lord's resurrection.

Ephesians, as we saw in our discussion of the resurrection and the church, goes a step further:

> But God, who is rich in mercy, out of the great love with which he loved us even when we were dead through our trespasses, made us alive together with Christ—by grace you have been saved—and *raised us up with him and seated us with him in the heavenly places* in Christ Jesus. (Eph 2:4-6)

Here believers are enthroned as well as raised up with Christ because they belong to the body of the risen and exalted Christ. Like Colossians, Ephesians is aware that the resurrection of the dead has not yet occurred. Its emphasis on the believer's association with Christ's resurrection and enthronement, however, provides believers with a powerful motivation for living a morally good life. For, if they are already associated with Christ's resurrection, they ought to live in a way that reflects this. And so Ephesians exhorts its readers:

> You were taught to put away your former way of life, your *old self*, corrupt and deluded by its lusts, and to be renewed in the spirit of your minds, and to clothe yourselves with the *new self*, created according to the likeness of God in true righteousness and holiness. (Eph 4:22-24)

The "new self" with which believers are to clothe themselves is the eschatological Adam, the New Man, who is the risen Lord Jesus Christ.

To sum up, the resurrection impacts the life of those who believe in the crucified and risen Christ. On the one hand, it enables them to live in the realm of the Spirit so that they enjoy a foretaste of resurrection life. On the other, it enables them to live a morally good life that accords with the new creation that has come about through Christ's resurrection.

## The Resurrection and the Renewal of Creation

Paul was firmly convinced that the resurrection of Jesus was not an isolated event—something that happened only to Jesus—but the beginning of the resurrection of the dead, and so the renewal of God's creation. Because Paul understood that Jesus' resurrection was the beginning of the general resurrection, he believed that Christ would soon return to gather the elect into God's kingdom. Although Paul was mistaken about the timing of the Parousia, his fundamental insight was on target, because if the resurrection of the dead has already begun in one man, God's Anointed One, then the end of the ages has begun. Consequently, believers live between two ages: the old aeon that Adam inaugurated by his transgression of God's commandment and the new aeon that the New Adam inaugurated by his obedience to God. Believers must still contend with the old aeon, but they know that it is running out and that the future—the only future that counts—belongs to God's new creation in Christ. The resurrection of Jesus Christ, then, is the beginning of God's new creation in which the creation, wounded by Adam's sin, is renewed and transformed by the New Adam's resurrection.

Paul draws out the relationship between Christ's resurrection and the resurrection of the justified in several texts. For example, he reminds the Thessalonians who are wondering about the fate of those who have died before the Lord's Parousia that those who have died in Christ will share in his victory at his Parousia: "But we do not want you to be uninformed, brothers and sisters, about those who have died, so that you may not grieve as others do who have no hope. *For since we believe that Jesus died and rose again, even so, through Jesus, God will bring with him those who have died*" (1 Thess 4:13-14). He makes a similar point when describing his apostolic ministry to the Corinthians: "So death is at work in us, but life in you. But just as we have the same spirit of faith that is in accordance with scripture—'I believed, and so I spoke'—we also believe, and so we speak, *because we know that the one who raised the Lord Jesus will raise us also with Jesus, and will bring us with you into his presence*" (2 Cor 4:12-14). Finally, in a statement of his own faith, he writes, "But our citizenship is in heaven, and it is from there that we are expecting a Savior, the Lord Jesus Christ. *He will transform the body of our humiliation that it may be conformed to the body of his glory*, by the power that also enables him to make all things subject to himself" (Phil 3:20-21). In all of these texts, Paul establishes an intimate relationship between the resurrection of Christ and the resurrection of those who believe in him.

In addition to inaugurating the general resurrection of the dead, the resurrection of Christ brings about the renewal of God's creation. Here there are several pertinent texts. The first is found in 1 Corinthians:

> [F]or as all die in Adam, so all will be made alive in Christ. But each in his own order: Christ the first fruits, then at his coming those who belong to Christ. Then comes the end, when he hands over the kingdom to God the Father, after he has destroyed every ruler and every authority and power. For he must reign until he has put all his enemies under his feet. The last enemy to be destroyed is death. For "God has put all things in subjection under his feet." But when it says, "All things are put in subjection," it is plain that this does not include the one who put all things in subjection under him. When all things are subjected to him, then the Son himself will also be subjected to the one who put all things in subjection under him, so that God may be all in all. (1 Cor 15:22-28)

Paul's premise is that Christ's resurrection is the beginning, the "first fruits," of the general resurrection that will occur when he returns. At the present time the risen Lord is reigning until all of his enemies are conquered. When the general resurrection takes place, the last and greatest enemy—Death—will be destroyed. Then the risen Lord will hand over the kingdom to God and, as an obedient Son, he will subject himself to the Father, so that God will be all in all. At the general resurrection of the dead, then, the whole of God's plan will be accomplished.

Paul is more specific about this plan in Romans 8. After reminding the Romans of the vital role the Spirit plays in their life, empowering them to live a morally good life and assuring them of their own resurrection, Paul describes the renewal of creation that will occur at the general resurrection of the dead:

> I consider that the sufferings of this present time are not worth comparing with the glory about to be revealed to us. For the *creation waits with eager longing for the revealing of the children of God*; for the creation was subjected to futility, not of its own will but by the will of the one who subjected it, in hope that the creation itself will be set free from its bondage to decay and will obtain the freedom of the glory of the children of God. We know that *the whole creation has been groaning in labor pains until now; and not only the creation, but we ourselves, who have the first fruits of the Spirit, groan inwardly while we wait for adoption, the redemption of our bodies*. (Rom 8:18-23)

Paul personifies creation by attributing self-consciousness to it. Creation has not been able to attain its purpose because of Adam's transgression. Because of this sin, God subjected creation to "futility," but not without hope. For creation "knows" that when God's children attain their "glory"—resurrection from the dead—it will share in this resurrection glory. This is why believers groan inwardly; they are awaiting "the redemption of their body," which will occur at the general resurrection of the dead.

In this magnificent passage Paul shows that the effects of Christ's resurrection are cosmic in scope; it is not just believers who will be saved but the whole of God's creation. For just as believers will be changed and transformed, so will the creation in which they live. Those who are risen with Christ will live in a renewed creation.

Toward the end of Romans 8, Paul summarizes the scope of God's redemptive plan in Christ in this way:

> For those whom he foreknew he also predestined *to be conformed to the image of his Son*, in order that he might be the firstborn within

a large family. And those whom he predestined he also called; and those whom he called he also justified; and those whom he justified *he also glorified.* (Rom 8:29-30)

In this brief statement the apostle points to the resurrection as the goal of the Christian life: the purpose of God's plan for humanity is to conform humanity to the image of the risen Christ, who is the image of God because he reflects God's own glory (2 Cor 3:18). Thus God calls, predestines, and justifies humanity for the purpose of glorifying it through the resurrection of the dead. Ephesians presents this in another way:

In him we have redemption through his blood, the forgiveness of our trespasses, according to the riches of his grace that he lavished on us. With all wisdom and insight he has made known to us the mystery of his will, according to his good pleasure that he set forth in Christ, as a plan for the fullness of time, *to gather up all things in him, things in heaven and things on earth.* (Eph 1:7-10)

God's redemptive plan in Christ has the entire cosmos in view. In God's way and in God's time all things will be renewed and taken up into the crucified and risen Lord.

To recapitulate, the resurrection of Christ is the beginning of the general resurrection from the dead through which the whole of God's creation will be renewed.

## Conclusion

As I noted at the outset of this chapter, there is a certain futility in any attempt to summarize what the Pauline letters say about the resurrection. The resurrection is not just a doctrine among doctrines; it is the linchpin for understanding all that the Pauline letters proclaim. The God in whom Paul believes is the God who raises the dead. The Christ whom he proclaims is the one whom God raised from the dead. The Spirit he experiences is the foretaste and guarantee of the resurrection. The church is the community of those who have come into existence by its Lord's resurrection. The moral life of the believer is empowered by the Spirit granted at the resurrection. And the final hope of the Christian is the resurrection. From start to finish, Pauline thought is determined by the resurrection of Christ and those who believe in him. Apart from the resurrection there is no Christian life; in the resurrection is the fullness of life.

## Note

1. F.-X. Durrwell (*The Resurrection: A Biblical Study*, trans. Rosemary Sheed [New York: Sheed and Ward, 1960], 130) writes of the risen Christ in this way: "We must take it that Christ will never grow any older than he was at the Resurrection, that his life remains new, that his body, newborn in the Spirit, never grows beyond the moment of his Easter birth and therefore that the Father's action in raising Christ continues eternally in its single moment."

# Chapter 5

# The Witness of Hebrews, 1 Peter, 1 John, and Revelation

While the gospels, Acts, and the Pauline writings provide us with the New Testament's major witness to the resurrection of Jesus, there are a number of other New Testament writings that also contribute to our understanding of Christ's resurrection and its meaning for those who believe in him. Among these the most important are Hebrews, 1 Peter, 1 John, and Revelation. These writings point to the resurrection as the goal of the Christian life. Encouraging and exhorting their readers to remain faithful to what they have believed, they promise that the glory Christ presently enjoys will be theirs if they endure with him to the end.

## Hebrews: Resurrection as Entrance into the Heavenly Sanctuary

On first reading, it appears that the Epistle to the Hebrews has little to contribute to our discussion of the resurrection. It focuses on the death of Christ rather than on his resurrection, and it does not contain the kind of resurrection formulas we encounter in the gospels and the Pauline letters. The only explicit reference to the

Lord's resurrection occurs at the end of Hebrews, where the unknown author of this treatise writes about "the God of peace, who brought back from the dead our Lord Jesus, the great shepherd of the sheep, by the blood of the eternal covenant" (13:20). At one point in its argument Hebrews even speaks of the resurrection of the dead as part of "the basic teaching about Christ" that it wants to go beyond so that its audience can attain perfection (6:1-2).[1]

A first reading of Hebrews, however, is not sufficient. Further readings of this sublime text reveal that the resurrection of Christ supports the entire argument of this treatise: namely, that Christ is a great high priest who has passed through the heavens to present the perfect sacrifice of his own blood for the forgiveness of sins, once and for all, in the heavenly temple of God. This action of Jesus, the great high priest, is not the work of a dead man; it is the priestly action of one who has entered into the heavenly sanctuary through his resurrection.

To uncover Hebrews' understanding of resurrection, it is not sufficient to look for explicit references to the resurrection of the dead. We must understand what undergirds the argument of Hebrews: that Jesus is a great high priest who has passed through the heavens and is now enthroned at God's right hand, where he makes intercession for those who believe in him. To show how Hebrews accomplishes this, I will explore its understanding of the resurrection in terms of Christ's high priesthood that makes it possible for believers to enter the Sabbath rest their high priest has already attained by his entrance into the heavenly sanctuary. In doing this, I will show that Hebrews presupposes Christ's resurrection when it speaks of his entrance into and enthronement in the heavenly sanctuary.[2] Furthermore, Hebrews points to the resurrection of believers when it reminds them of the Sabbath rest and the heavenly city that awaits them if they follow the "pioneer of their salvation" (2:10).

In summary, although Hebrews does not speak explicitly about the resurrection of Christ apart from 13:20, it has a great deal to say about his entrance into the heavenly sanctuary where he is enthroned at the right hand of God. In doing so, Hebrews presupposes the resurrection since this entrance and enthronement could not have happened if Christ had not been raised from the dead.

### Christ's Resurrection as Entrance into the Heavenly Sanctuary

The central theme of Hebrews is that Christ is a high priest who entered the heavenly sanctuary where he offered himself as a sacrifice for sins, once and for all. In developing this theme, Hebrews presents its readers with a new way to think about their Lord's death and resurrection: namely, Christ's death was the act of a high priest who offered himself in sacrifice, and his resurrection was his entrance into the heavenly sanctuary to present this sacrifice.

Hebrews is keenly aware that Jesus was not qualified to minister as a priest in the temple of Jerusalem since he did not belong to the priestly tribe of Levi. Therefore, it argues that his priesthood was of another kind: he was a high priest according to the order of Melchizedek.

To establish this understanding of Christ's priesthood, Hebrews makes use of Psalms 2 and 110. Both psalms belong to the category of royal psalms and were addressed to the Israelite king on the day of his coronation. For the early church, however, they were prophetic utterances of David that spoke of the Messiah. Accordingly, the church understood Psalm 2:7 as a prophecy of Christ's resurrection: "You [Christ] are my Son; / today [the day of the resurrection] I have begotten you." In a similar way, it interpreted Psalm 110:1 as a prophecy of Christ's heavenly enthronement as Messiah after his resurrection: "Sit at my right hand / until I make your enemies your footstool."

But Hebrews goes further by including Psalm 110:4 as well: "You are a priest forever, / according to the order of Melchizedek." By including this verse, Hebrews argues that Christ, who was declared to be God's Son (Ps 2:7) and enthroned at God's right hand (Ps 110:1) on the day of his resurrection, was, on that day, also made a high priest according to the order of Melchizedek (Ps 110:4).

Hebrews returns to these psalm texts again and again, explicitly and implicitly. For example, in its exquisite introduction it alludes to Psalm 110:1: "When he had made purification for sins, he sat down *at the right hand of the Majesty on high*" (1:3). At the beginning of the long list of scriptural quotations in 1:5-13, Hebrews quotes Psalm

2:7 and concludes with a quotation from Psalm 110:1. Then in 5:5 it employs both psalms to establish Christ's high priesthood:

> So also Christ did not glorify himself in becoming a high priest, but was appointed by the one who said to him,
> "You are my Son,
> today I have begotten you" [Ps 2:7];
> as he says also in another place,
> "You are a priest forever,
> according to the order of Melchizedek" [Ps 110:4].

In this text Hebrews draws a relationship between the priesthood of Christ and his resurrection that can be stated in this way: in virtue of his resurrection Christ was appointed a high priest according to the order of Melchizedek.

According to Hebrews there was need for a new priesthood because the sacrifices of the Levitical priesthood could not cleanse the consciences of those who offered them. Its priests offered the blood of animals that was incapable of bringing people to perfection and dealing with their sins once and for all. Therefore, Hebrews argues, there was need for a new priesthood according to the order of Melchizedek. Hebrews alludes to the role of the resurrection in this priesthood when it compares the priesthood of Christ and the Levitical priesthood:

> Furthermore, the former priests were many in number, because they were prevented by death from continuing in office; but *he holds his priesthood permanently, because he continues forever.* Consequently he is able for all time to save those who approach God through him, *since he always lives to make intercession for them.* (7:23-25)

Whereas the old priesthood needed to be replenished as each generation died, the high priesthood of Christ endures forever since he lives forever in virtue of his resurrection from the dead.

But when did Christ become a high priest according to the order of Melchizedek? For Hebrews the answer is found in its understanding Christ's death and resurrection. Drawing on the imagery of the Day of Atonement (see Leviticus 16), the one day each year when the high priest entered the holiest part of the sanctuary, the holy of holies, to sanctify the people, Hebrews says that Christ entered the true holy of holies, the very sanctuary of heaven, with his own blood rather than with the blood of goats and calves:

> But when Christ came as a high priest of the good things that have come, then through the greater and perfect tent (not made with hands, that is, not of this creation), he entered once for all into the Holy Place, not with the blood of goats and calves, but with his own blood, thus obtaining eternal redemption. (9:11-12)

It was through his death and resurrection, then, that Christ entered the heavenly sanctuary and was enthroned at God's right hand as high priest according to the order of Melchizedek. Unlike the priests of the old covenant who offered many sacrifices, this priest offered himself in sacrifice once and for all and then took his seat at the right hand of God (10:12). Living forever, he now makes intercession for those who approach God through him (7:25).

Hebrews's understanding of the resurrection is intimately related to its theology of the high priesthood of Christ. Jesus' death and resurrection was the redemptive act by which he entered the sanctuary of heaven with the sacrifice of his own blood and was declared Son of God and high priest according to the order of Melchizedek. The sacrifice that he brought into heaven was the sacrifice of his life, and his entrance into the heavenly sanctuary was his resurrection.

### The Believer's Resurrection as Entrance into God's Sabbath Rest and the Heavenly City

Just as Hebrews speaks of Christ's resurrection in terms of his entrance into the heavenly sanctuary, so it speaks of the resurrection of those who believe in him in terms of entrance into God's Sabbath rest and in terms of entering into God's heavenly city. For Hebrews Jesus is "the pioneer and perfecter of our faith, who for the sake of the joy that was set before him endured the cross, disregarding its shame, and has taken his seat at the right hand of the throne of God" (12:2). He is the one who has been made "perfect through sufferings" (2:10), and having been made perfect he is now "the source of eternal salvation" for all who believe in him (5:9).

At the outset of its great discourse on the high priesthood of Christ, Hebrews employs Psalm 8 to remind its audience of the destiny that lies before it (2:5-9). Crowned with glory and honor, humanity is destined to rule over the world to come. That humanity will be crowned with glory and honor is already seen in the glory and honor that Jesus, the pioneer of their salvation, has obtained:

> As it is, we do not yet see everything in subjection to them [human beings], but we do see Jesus, who for a little while was made lower than the angels, now crowned with glory and honor because of the suffering of death, so that by the grace of God he might taste death for everyone. (2:8-9)

The destiny of Jesus, then, is the destiny of those who believe in him. What he has attained, they will obtain if they remain faithful to him.

After assuring believers of the destiny that lies before them, Hebrews employs the story of Israel wandering in the wilderness to exhort its audience not to harden their hearts as the wilderness generation did (3:7–4:7). Beginning with an extended quotation from Psalm 95, Hebrews recounts how God was angry for forty years with that generation of people who heard his voice but hardened their hearts in disobedience. Consequently, God declared they would not enter his rest.

To be sure, a new generation entered the Promised Land, but for Hebrews the promise of entering God's Sabbath rest is greater than entering into the land. Therefore Hebrews concludes that the promise of entering God's Sabbath rest still remains to be fulfilled, and it exhorts its audience in this way:

> For if Joshua had given them rest, God would not speak later about another day. So then, a sabbath rest still remains for the people of God; for those who enter God's rest also cease from their labors as God did from his. Let us therefore make every effort to enter that rest, so that no one may fall through such disobedience as theirs. (4:8-11)

At this point in its argument, Hebrews does not explain what this Sabbath rest is. But as the discourse develops, it becomes clear that it is entrance into the heavenly sanctuary that Jesus has already entered, the new and eternal city built by God.

In chapter 11, after its lengthy discussion of Christ's priesthood, Hebrews presents its audience with a stirring exhortation to remain faithful to what it has received. Drawing on examples of faith from the history of Israel, it reminds its audience of what Israel's ancestors hoped to attain. Abraham was looking forward "to the city that has foundations, whose architect and builder is God" (11:10). Others desired "a better country, that is, a heavenly one. Therefore God is not ashamed to be called their God; indeed, he has prepared a city for them" (11:16). Abraham was willing to sacrifice Isaac because he considered that God could raise the dead and so he received Isaac back as a kind of parable pointing to Jesus' resurrection (11:19). Women also received their dead back in resurrection, and others underwent torture in hope of "a better resurrection," namely, the resurrection Jesus would make possible (11:35).

After this discourse, Hebrews reminds its audience that they are no longer approaching the fearsome sight of Mount Sinai that the wilderness generation saw:

> But you have come to Mount Zion and to *the city of the living God*, the heavenly Jerusalem, and to innumerable angels in festal gathering, and to *the assembly of the firstborn* who are enrolled in heaven, and to God the judge of all, and to the spirits of the righteous made perfect, and to Jesus, the mediator of a new covenant, and to the sprinkled blood that speaks a better word than the blood of Abel. (12:22-24)

This city of the living God for which their ancestors were hoping is the assembly of the "firstborn," that is, the assembly of those who have been raised from the dead as was Jesus, the firstborn from the dead (see 1:6).

To sum up, entrance into God's Sabbath rest is entrance into the heavenly city, the assembly of the firstborn from the dead. Those who enter into God's Sabbath rest have been raised from the dead because they belong to the city of God, the assembly of the firstborn.

### Resurrection in Hebrews

Although the metaphors Hebrews employs when speaking about the effects of the resurrection are different from what we encounter in the rest of the New Testament, they share affinities with what we find in the gospels and the Pauline Epistles. In the Synoptic Gospels the goal of salvation is expressed in terms of entering the kingdom of God. In the Fourth Gospel it is expressed in terms of entering into eternal life, and in the Pauline Epistles in terms of the general resurrection of the dead. In every instance, it is a matter of obtaining what Jesus has already attained. And so it is with Hebrews. By entering into God's Sabbath rest, the heavenly city of God, believers enter into the heavenly sanctuary where their high priest makes continual intercession for them. This entrance into God's Sabbath rest, the heavenly city, is the result of being raised from the dead as well as another way of expressing what is meant by resurrection from the dead. For example, when contemporary believers talk about their salvation in terms of "heaven," they are implicitly speaking of resurrection from the dead in view of the fact that entrance into heaven is the result of being raised from the dead. And so it is with Hebrews. Christ's entrance into the heavenly sanctuary and the believer's entrance into God's Sabbath rest can be viewed in two ways: the result of the resurrection from the dead as well as a way of speaking about the resurrection of the dead.

## 1 Peter: Resurrection as a New Birth to a Living Hope

In his magisterial commentary on 1 Peter my revered teacher, Paul J. Achtemeier, notes that the theological structure of 1 Peter "is shaped by the categories of past, present, and future, used in two sets of parallels."[3] In the first set there is a parallel between the *past* of Christ and the *present* of the Christian: just as Christ suffered in the *past*, so the Christian is suffering in the *present*. In the second set there is a parallel between the *present* of Christ and the *future* of the Christian: just as Christ is glorified in the *present*, so the Christian will be glorified in the *future*. These parallels can be presented in this way.

| | |
|---|---|
| The *past suffering* of Christ | The *present suffering* of the Christian |
| The *present glory* of Christ | The *future glory* of the Christian |

Given this theological structure, I will examine what 1 Peter teaches about the resurrection under two headings: (1) the suffering and glory of Christ, (2) the suffering and glory of those who believe in him.

## *The Suffering and Glory of Christ*

First Peter presents its readers with a rich Christology that highlights the past suffering and present glory of Christ. For example, at the outset of this letter Peter reminds his audience that the salvation that will be theirs was already announced by the prophets when the Spirit of Christ—already at work in them—"testified in advance to the sufferings destined for Christ and the subsequent glory" (1:11). That "subsequent glory" was Christ's resurrection from the dead, as is apparent from what Peter writes a few verses later:

> He was destined before the foundation of the world, but was revealed at the end of the ages for your sake. Through him you have come to trust in God, *who raised him from the dead and gave him glory*, so that your faith and hope are set on God. (1:20-21)

At the outset of this letter, then, Peter reminds his readers of the pattern of Christ's life, which should be the pattern of their own lives: suffering now, glory later.

The theme of Christ's past suffering plays a major role in this letter. In his exhortation to Christian slaves, for example, Peter exhorts them to endure their present suffering, even if it is unjust, just as Christ endured his sufferings:

> For to this you have been called, because *Christ also suffered for you, leaving you an example*, so that you should follow in his steps.
> "He committed no sin,
>     and no deceit was found in his mouth."
> When he was abused, he did not return abuse; *when he suffered, he did not threaten*; but he entrusted himself to the one who judges justly. He

himself bore our sins in his body on the cross, so that, free from sins, we might live for righteousness; by his wounds you have been healed. For you were going astray like sheep, but now you have returned to the shepherd and guardian of your souls. (1 Peter 2:21-25)

Although Peter addresses this exhortation to Christian slaves, it is intended for all. Speaking to the wider community he writes, "Now who will harm you if you are eager to do what is good? *But even if you do suffer for doing what is right, you are blessed.* Do not fear what they fear, and do not be intimidated" (3:13-14). Providing the entire community with the same motivation he gave Christian slaves, he says,

> For *Christ also suffered* for sins once for all, the righteous for the unrighteous, in order to bring you to God. *He was put to death in the flesh, but made alive in the spirit,* in which also he went and made a proclamation to the spirits in prison, who in former times did not obey, when God waited patiently in the days of Noah, during the building of the ark, in which a few, that is, eight persons, were saved through water. And baptism, which this prefigured, now saves you—not as a removal of dirt from the body, but as an appeal to God for a good conscience, *through the resurrection of Jesus Christ,* who has gone into heaven and is at the right hand of God, with angels, authorities, and powers made subject to him. (3:18-22)

In this text Peter brings his theology of Christ's past suffering and present glory to full expression: Christ was put to death in the past because he suffered for our sins, but now he enjoys resurrection glory because God brought him to new life in the spirit by raising him from the dead so that Christ is presently enthroned at the right hand of God with the angelic powers subject to him.

### The Suffering and Glory of Those Who Believe in Christ

Since the pattern of Christ's life is the pattern of the believer's life, 1 Peter applies the pattern of suffering and glory that characterized the life of Christ to the life of those who believe in him. But rather than starting with the suffering that his audience is presently enduring, he reminds them of their new situation and the future glory that awaits them.

He tells them that they have been given "a new birth into a living hope through the resurrection of Jesus Christ from the dead" (1:3). This new birth assures them of a heavenly inheritance, which is their salvation (1:4-5). They have been "born anew . . . through the living and enduring word of God" (1:23). They are like "newborn infants" who are growing into salvation (2:2). They are "living stones" who are being built into a "spiritual house" (2:5). Formerly they were not a people, but now they are God's people (2:10).

This new birth took place at their baptism, which was prefigured in the story of Noah. Just as Noah and his family were saved in the ark through the waters of the flood, so believers are protected from God's judgment by the waters of baptism that provide them with a "good conscience" before God "through the resurrection of Jesus Christ" (3:21). It is Christ's resurrection, then, that gives baptism its saving power and enables the baptized to stand before God with a good conscience, a theme we found in Hebrews 9:14 in regard to Christ's death.

Although believers have experienced a new birth through Christ's resurrection, their present situation is one of suffering because they are Christians. Accordingly, after describing the new life that belongs to those who believe in Christ (1:3–2:10), Peter exhorts his readers to endure their present suffering in light of the future glory that will be theirs if they live according to the pattern Christ manifested in his own life (2:11–4:11).

### Resurrection in 1 Peter

The distinctive contribution of 1 Peter to our discussion of the resurrection is the manner in which it employs the suffering and resurrection of Christ to encourage believers to endure the sufferings they are presently enduring. For 1 Peter suffering and resurrection are intimately related: suffering is the prelude to resurrection glory, and resurrection glory is the inheritance of those who suffer for Christ. Peter can speak of this intimate connection between present suffering and future resurrection glory because he is "a witness of the sufferings of Christ, as well as one who shares in the glory to be revealed" (5:1). In calling himself a witness to Christ's suffering, Peter is not so much claiming to have been an eyewitness to the Lord's sufferings as he is affirming that he also suffers on account of Christ. Writing as a fellow Christian, he proclaims his solidarity with believers who are suffering because of their faith in Christ in hope of the glory that will be theirs at the resurrection.

First Peter's theology of the resurrection can be viewed in terms of the present and the future. In terms of the present the resurrection brings a new birth through the living word of God proclaimed in baptism: believers are born anew and given a heavenly inheritance. In terms of the future, the resurrection provides believers with the assurance of final salvation if they follow the example of Christ, who suffered in view of the glory that would be his at the resurrection.

## 1 John: Resurrection and Incarnation

There are no explicit references to the resurrection of Jesus in First John.[4] Like the Fourth Gospel, this letter focuses its theology through the prism of the incarnation. Nevertheless, everything that 1 John proclaims, including its profound faith in the incarnation, presupposes a prior understanding of, and faith in, the resurrection. Without the resurrection there would be no talk of eternal life; there would be no confession that Jesus is the Christ; there would be no anointing of the Spirit; there would be no union with Christ. Thus, while the incarnation is the prism through which this letter filters its theology, it is the resurrection that gives birth to the incarnational theology that characterizes this letter and the Fourth Gospel. For, if death had conquered Jesus once and for all, if God had not raised Jesus from the dead, there would be no faith in the incarnation. The distinctive contribution of 1 John to our study of the resurrection, then, is the manner in which it interprets the resurrection through the lens of the incarnation. This can be seen in the way 1 John insists that believers have eternal life, that Jesus is the Christ, and that believers are God's children.

## *The Word of Life*

The theme of life/eternal life plays a central role in this letter. The author of 1 John (whom I will call "John") and those associated with him proclaim "the word of life" (1:1). This life was made visible to them. They "have seen it and testify to it," and they proclaim "eternal life" to the recipients of this letter (1:2) so that they may have fellowship with them.

John exhorts the community of believers to abide in the message of life they have heard from the beginning so that they will abide in the Son and in the Father. He reminds them of the promise of eternal life made to them (2:24-25). They have already "passed from death to life because [they] love one another" (3:14). The way they came to know this love was through Jesus, who laid down his life for them (3:16). It is God who has given them eternal life, a life grounded in his Son so that whoever possesses the Son possesses life (5:11-12).

Although 1 John never explicitly uses the language of resurrection, it is difficult to conceive of the life of which it speaks apart from the resurrection. For while the "word of life" is certainly the message about the incarnate one, the message is ultimately about the one whom the Father raised from the dead. This eternal life is the life that originates through faith in Jesus the incarnate one, and it finds fulfillment in resurrection from the dead as is apparent from the Fourth Gospel:

> Indeed, just as the Father raises the dead and gives them life, so also the Son gives life to whomever he wishes. (John 5:21)

> Those who eat my flesh and drink my blood have eternal life, and I will raise them up on the last day. (John 6:54)

## *Jesus is the Christ*

Since the life of which 1 John speaks is the eternal life made possible by the resurrection of the one the Father has sent into the world, the source of this life is Jesus Christ. This is why 1 John concludes, "And we know that the Son of God has come and has given us understanding so that we may know him who is true; and we are in him who is true, in his Son Jesus Christ. *He is the true God and eternal life*" (5:20). There is a strong insistence throughout this letter, therefore, that *Jesus*, the human one in whom the eternal Word of God was incarnate, is the Christ.

Aware that there are some who have left the community of believers and deny this confession, John identifies such people as those who deny the truth and so reject the message of life the gospel proclaims: "*Who is the liar but the one who denies that Jesus is the Christ? This is the antichrist, the one who denies the Father and the Son. No one who denies the Son has the Father; everyone who confesses the Son has the Father also*" (2:22-23). Those who confess that *Jesus* has "come *in the flesh*" belong to God (4:2). And everyone who believes that *Jesus* is the Christ is born of God (5:1).[5]

The central christological confession of 1 John is that *Jesus* is the Christ, the Son of God. The manner in which 1 John insists that the human one, *Jesus*, is the Christ, the Son of God, comes from its understanding of the incarnation—the Word of God was made flesh in Jesus. But its insistence that *Jesus* is the Christ presupposes the resurrection, that moment when the Father glorified his Son as the Christ. To be sure, Jesus identifies himself as the Messiah in his conversation with the Samaritan woman (John 4:25-26); and in his high priestly prayer he speaks of himself as Jesus Christ (John 17:3). For 1 John, however, "*Jesus* is the Christ" is a confessional formula made possible by the resurrection, and this confession now identifies those who possess eternal life. For if God did not raise Jesus from the dead, it is difficult to understand why or how the community of believers could confess *Jesus* as the Christ. Consequently, even though 1 John does not explicitly refer to the resurrection, it surely presupposes it.

### Begotten by God

According to 1 John everyone who believes that *Jesus* is the Christ "has been born of God" (5:1), and those born of God do not sin because "God's seed abides in them" (3:9). Those born of God love one another (4:7), and they have conquered the world through their faith (5:4). They are God's children because of the new life they have through their confession that *Jesus* is the Christ.

But 1 John is aware that even though believers are God's children, what they will be has not yet been revealed. And so John writes,

"Beloved, we are God's children now; what we will be has not yet been revealed. What we do know is this: *when he is revealed, we will be like him*, for we will see him as he is. And all who have this hope in him purify themselves, just as he is pure" (3:2-3).

In these verses 1 John manifests an eschatology similar to that of Philippians 3:21: "*He will transform the body of our humiliation that it may be conformed to the body of his glory*, by the power that also enables him to make all things subject to himself." At the present time believers experience something of resurrection life because of their faith in *Jesus* the Christ, but in the future they will be like the one in whom they believe; they will be changed and transformed by the power of his resurrection. Although 1 John does not explicitly refer to the resurrection in the way Philippians does, it makes a similar point: what Christ is, believers will be.

### Resurrection in 1 John

Although 1 John never explicitly refers to the resurrection of Christ or of those who believe in him, what it says about eternal life, what it says about *Jesus* being the Christ, and what it says about believers being God's children presupposes a prior understanding of the resurrection. This understanding, however, is filtered through 1 John's theology of the incarnation so that the distinctive contribution of 1 John to a theology of the resurrection is the incarnation, which is revealed through the resurrection.

John's contribution to an understanding of the resurrection can be summarized in this way. Although the incarnation is chronologically prior to the resurrection, *it is the resurrection that reveals the incarnation*, and it is in light of the resurrection that Johannine theology understands that the risen one is the incarnate one. Having come to this understanding of Jesus through the resurrection, John proclaims what God has done in light of the incarnation. In sum, John's contribution to an understanding of the resurrection is the incarnation.

## The Book of Revelation: Resurrection as Victory

The resurrection of Jesus Christ and of those who witness to him plays a central role in the book of Revelation. In the opening chapters of this prophecy, the risen Christ addresses the seven churches to which this book is addressed. Then, in chapter 5, there is a second portrayal of the risen Christ as the Lamb who opens the scroll. Finally, throughout this prophecy there are several descriptions of faithful witnesses to the Lamb who have already attained to the resurrection and now await God's final victory.

The book of Revelation, however, is not a speculative work; it is a prophetic message from God given to John by Jesus Christ to strengthen Christians who are presently enduring, or about to endure, persecution. What the book of Revelation affirms about the resurrection, then, is intended to assure believers that if they remain faithful witnesses to Jesus, they will share in his resurrection just as those who have already died because of their witness to Jesus presently share in his resurrection. Like the Epistle to the Hebrews and 1 Peter, the book of Revelation draws a correlation between what happened to Jesus and what is presently happening to those who believe in him: just as Jesus suffered and died because of his witness to God and was raised from the dead, so those who suffer and die because of their witness to him will be raised from the dead.

### *The Risen Jesus*

The book of Revelation presents listeners with two descriptions of the risen Christ: (1) a portrayal of him as one like a Son of Man, reminiscent of the glorious figure described in the book of Daniel, and (2) as a Lamb that appears to have been slaughtered but lives nonetheless. In the first description, the risen Christ is in the midst of the seven churches to which this prophecy is directed. In the second, he is in heaven in the throne room of God where he opens the scroll that foretells what must happen. Since both descriptions of the risen one are different, it is clear they are to be taken figuratively rather than literally.

In the first description (1:12-16) the risen Christ is standing in the midst of seven golden lampstands that represent the seven churches to which this prophecy is directed. That he stands in the midst of these lampstands points to his presence to the churches, even if they are not aware of it. He is described as "one like a son of man" (Dan 7:13, RSV), wearing a long robe and a golden sash

(Dan 10:5). His head and hair are white as wool (Dan 7:9),[6] his eyes like flames of fire, his feet like burnished bronze, and his voice like the sound of rushing waters (Dan 10:6). In his hands he holds seven stars that represent the angels that guard the seven churches. A two-edged sword, which is the Word of God, comes from his mouth, and his face shines with the brightness of the sun. He identifies himself as risen and alive: "I am the first and the last, and the living one. I was dead, and see, I am alive forever and ever; and I have the keys of Death and of Hades" (Rev 1:17-18).

Many of these traits of the risen Christ are repeated at the beginning of the messages he addresses to the seven churches, thereby reinforcing the description of the risen Christ as the one "who holds the seven stars" (2:1), "the first and the last," the one who died and "came to life" (2:8), the one with "the sharp two-edged sword" (2:12), the Son of God whose eyes are like fiery flame and whose feet are like polished brass (2:18). Furthermore, all of the rewards he promises to those who endure to the end allude to the resurrection life they will enjoy: "the tree of life" (2:7), protection from "the second death" (2:11), "the hidden manna" (2:17), "authority over the nations" (2:26), "the book of life" (3:5), the temple of God, "the new Jerusalem" (3:12), the throne (3:21).

While this description enables those who hear it to "imagine" the risen Christ, its primary purpose is to assure the seven churches that the risen Lord is in their midst and to draw a relationship between him and the one like a son of man described in the book of Daniel. Just as God vindicated the one like a son of man, so God has vindicated Jesus. And just as God vindicated Jesus, so God will vindicate those who remain faithful to Christ. As the risen one, he is present to the churches in their tribulations, speaking the powerful word of God.

The second description of the risen Christ is different from the first in two ways. First, it takes place in the throne room of God rather than on earth. Second, the risen Lord is portrayed in the figure of an animal rather than as one like a son of man. At first the risen Christ is portrayed as "the Lion of the tribe of Judah, the Root of David" (5:5). Then, without warning, "a Lamb standing as if it had been slaughtered" (5:6) replaces the Lion of Judah. Whereas the figure of the Lion portrays Christ as a powerful messianic figure of

David's line (Gen 49:9), the Lamb portrays him as a sacrificial victim, the Lamb of God (see John 1:19, 36), who conquers through death rather than through power and might.

The Lamb who was slaughtered but now lives represents the crucified and risen Christ who is worthy to open the scroll that no one in heaven or on earth is able to open. When the Lamb takes the seal from the One who is seated on the throne, the twenty-four elders worship him as they worship God and sing a new song to the Lamb:

> You are worthy to take the scroll
> > and to open its seals,
> for you were slaughtered and by your blood you ransomed for God
> > saints from every tribe and language and people and nation;
> you have made them to be a kingdom and priests serving our God,
> > and they will reign on earth. (5:9-10)

Then the angels and living creatures sing to the Lamb:

> Worthy is the Lamb that was slaughtered
> to receive power and wealth and wisdom and might
> and honor and glory and blessing! (5:12)

Finally, every creature in heaven and on earth sings to *both* God and the Lamb:

> To the one seated on the throne and to the Lamb
> be blessing and honor and glory and might
> forever and ever! (5:13)

The final song, which is sung to *both* God and the Lamb, highlights the status of the risen Christ who is worthy of the same worship given to God. Having been slaughtered by human powers, he has been exalted by divine power.

### The Risen Saints

In addition to its describing the risen Christ, there are several occasions when the book of Revelation describes those who have already attained the resurrection because, like the Lamb who was slaughtered but now lives, they conquered through death.

The first of these occasions occurs when the Lamb opens the fifth seal and John sees under the altar in heaven the souls of those who had been "slaughtered for the word of God and for the testimony they had given" (6:9). While the description of them as "souls" gives the impression that they are disembodied spirits who are under God's altar waiting for the general resurrection of the dead, the fact that each of them is "given a white robe" (6:11) indicates otherwise. They have already conquered and so they enjoy resurrection life.[7]

A second instance can be found in 7:9-17, when John sees "a great multitude that no one could count" (7:9). They are standing around the throne of the Lamb, robed in white, like the "souls" under the altar, which could indicate they are the same group. John is told these "are they who have come out of the great ordeal; they have washed their robes and made them white in the blood of the Lamb. / For this reason they are before the throne of God, / and worship him day and night within his temple, / and the one who is seated on the throne will shelter them" (7:14-15). Like the souls under the altar, they have attained resurrection glory.

A third example occurs in 14:1-4, when John sees the Lamb standing on Mount Zion with the 144,000 who had previously been sealed by God's angel (7:1-8). They now sing a new song before the throne of God that no one could sing except the 144,000 "who had been redeemed from the earth" (14:3) as the "first fruits for God and the Lamb" (14:4). The 144,000 who had been protected by God's seal have attained to the resurrection of the dead.

Finally, toward the end of the book of Revelation, after the beast and its armies have been defeated, Satan is bound and those who have been martyred for Christ come to life and reign with him for a thousand years. John calls this resurrection of the martyrs "the first resurrection," noting that the rest of the dead will come to life after the millennium (20:5, 12-13). It is difficult to integrate what Revelation says about the millennium with what we have noted thus far, unless we make some sort of distinction between the resurrection life that believers already enjoy with the Lamb in heaven and a resurrection of the dead at the end when all will be judged.[8]

### Resurrection in Revelation

The book of Revelation does not so much provide us with new teaching on resurrection as it witnesses to the reality of the resurrection through its portrayals of Christ and those who have remained faithful to him. It affirms that Christ is "the faithful witness, the firstborn of the dead" (1:5). He was dead and now he is "alive forever and ever," holding the keys of death and Hades (1:18). To those who are faithful until death, he gives "the crown of life" (2:10). The eternal life that Christ has attained, believers will attain.

## A Common Theme

Hebrews, 1 Peter, 1 John, and the book of Revelation express their understanding of the resurrection in different ways. In Hebrews resurrection is entrance into the heavenly sanctuary; in 1 Peter it is a new birth; in 1 John it is eternal life; and in the book of Revelation it is entrance into the new Jerusalem and the throne room of God where God and the Lamb are worshiped.

Despite these different ways of expressing their understanding of the resurrection, each of these writings makes a similar point: *the victory the risen Christ presently enjoys is the victory those who believe in him will enjoy if they persevere until the end.* Just as Jesus the high priest entered the heavenly sanctuary through his death and resurrection, so will those who follow him in the way of faith. Just as Jesus was glorified after he suffered, so will those who believe in him. Just as Jesus enjoys the fullness of God's life, so will those who continue in their confession of him as the Christ. Just as the Lamb who was slain received new life because of his faithful witness to God, so will those who faithfully witness to him.

In every instance there is a correlation between the risen Christ and those who believe in him: what he is, they will become if they remain faithful to him. Thus, while resurrection is a gift, God's sheer grace, it is a gift that requires a response from those who hope to attain it.

Having examined what the New Testament says about the resurrection of Jesus and those who believe in him, it is time to summarize its central teaching about Jesus' resurrection and the resurrection of his followers.

# Notes

1. F. F. Bruce (*The Epistle to the Hebrews: The English Text with Introduction, Exposition and Notes* [Grand Rapids: Eerdmans, 1964], lvi) summarizes the situation when he writes, "It is because of his concentration on the priestly aspect of Christ's work that our author has so much to say of His death and exaltation, but so little of His resurrection. The two principle moments in the great sin-offering of Old Testament times were the shedding of the victim's blood in the court of the sanctuary and the presentation of its blood inside the sanctuary. In the antitype these two moments were seen to correspond to the death of Christ on the cross and His appearance at the right hand of God. In this pattern the resurrection, as generally proclaimed in the apostolic preaching, finds no separate place."

2. William Lane (*Hebrews 1–8*, Word Biblical Commentary, vol. 47 [Dallas: Word Books Publisher, 1991], 16), commenting on Hebrews 1:3, makes a similar point when he writes, "Christians were familiar with the notion of the Son's session at God's right hand from creedal confessions and hymns. They would recognize immediately that the reference was to Christ's exaltation after his resurrection. This may explain why there is so little direct appeal to the fact of Jesus' resurrection in Hebrews (cf. 13:20). In v. 3 and elsewhere, an allusion to the position of God's right hand apparently served as an inclusive reference to Jesus' resurrection, ascension, and continuing exaltation."

3. Paul J. Achtemeier, *1 Peter: A Commentary on First Peter*, ed. Eldon Jay Epp, Hermeneia (Minneapolis: Fortress, 1996), 68.

4. The recent work of Matthew D. Jensen (*Affirming the Resurrection of the Incarnate Christ: A Reading of 1 John*, SNTSMS 153 [Cambridge: Cambridge University Press, 2012]) is an attempt to address the neglected question of the resurrection in 1 John.

5. I have italicized "Jesus" in order to show the emphasis the Epistle wants to convey: one must believe that *Jesus*, the human one in whom the Word was incarnate, is the Christ.

6. This is how the Ancient of Day, God, is described in the book of Daniel. The fact that the risen Lord is described in this way, then, is significant.

7. This point is made by Michael Labahn in his article, "The Imagery of Death and Life in the Book of Revelation," pp. 319–42 in *Resurrection of the Dead: Biblical Traditions in Dialogue*, BETL 240 (Leuven: Peeters, 2012).

8. The book of Revelation seems to presuppose that although the faithful dead already enjoy resurrection life with the Lamb, there will be a resurrection of the just and the unjust when all will be judged in a public way.

# The Mystery of the Resurrection

## The Resurrection as an Act of God

Any attempt to understand the meaning of the resurrection of Jesus and his followers must begin with an acknowledgment that the resurrection is an act of God. It is not something that human beings do; it is not something that human beings can do for themselves. Even though the gospels speak of the Son of Man rising from the dead (Mark 9:31), Jesus did not raise himself from the dead. Inasmuch as he is the incarnate Son of God, the one who shared in our human condition in all things but sin, Jesus *was raised from the dead* by the power of God. This is the constant witness of the New Testament that is firmly attested in the early creedal formula that was handed on to Paul, and that he in turn handed on to the Corinthians (1 Cor 15:3-5). To say that Jesus and his followers are raised from the dead is to affirm that the resurrection of the dead is an act of God's power, an act of unmerited grace.

Paul describes the power of this act when he prays that his audience will know the "immeasurable greatness" of the power that God displayed when he raised Jesus from the dead "and seated him at his right hand in the heavenly places, far above all rule and authority and power and dominion, and above every name that is named, not only in this age but also in the age to come. And he has put all things under his feet and has made him the head over all things for the church, which is his body, the fullness of him who fills all in all" (Eph 1:19-23).

By raising Jesus from the dead, God asserted his power in a definitive way over every malevolent power, whether on earth or in heaven. By raising Jesus from the dead, God overcame the cosmic powers of Sin and Death that ruled over humanity. This is why, in the light of Jesus' resurrection, Paul affirms that nothing can separate the justified from God's love in Christ Jesus (Rom 8:38-39). Just as God saved his Son from the powers of Sin and Death, so those who follow Jesus in the way of faith will be raised from the dead, never to die again.

The Gospel of Mark affirms that the resurrection was an act of God when it notes that "the stone, which was very large, had already *been rolled back*" (Mark 16:4). While this may appear to be an incidental detail, its purpose is to point out that the resurrection of Jesus was an act of God. Human beings put Jesus to death, buried him, and sealed his tomb with a massive stone, but God gave him new life by raising him from the dead. A similar point is made in the many contrast formulas we found in the speeches of Peter and Paul in the Acts of the Apostles: "this man, handed over to you according to the definite plan and foreknowledge of God, you crucified and killed by the hands of those outside the law. But God raised him up, having freed him from death" (Acts 2:23-24). Human beings did what they could to destroy Jesus and discredit his proclamation of the kingdom, but God overruled what they did by a powerful act of forgiving grace.

To say that the resurrection from the dead is an act of God is to affirm that Jesus was raised from the dead by the transcendent power of God who alone gives and restores life. Just as creation is an act of God beyond the power of human beings, so the resurrection of the dead is an act of God beyond the power of human beings, for it is a new creation, a calling into new life. The crucified Jesus had been put to death by his enemies. Having experienced the full power of death, he was, in the view of the world, vanquished by death. In the eyes of his enemies, he no longer dwelt in the land of the living. But through the resurrection of the dead he entered into a new life that brought him into perfect communion with God. This is why the resurrection of the dead is an act of God, for only God could give Jesus such life, only God could give Jesus resurrection life. Only God could bring Jesus into a new creation.

## The Resurrection as a New Creation

By raising Jesus from the dead, God inaugurated a new creation, for in the person of the crucified and risen Christ the old creation of sin and death was condemned and put to death and a new creation of grace and life was achieved in the eschatological Adam, the risen Christ. Although this new creation is not yet fully visible, as the Epistle to the Hebrews reminds us, we do see the risen Christ "crowned with glory and honor" (Heb 2:9). In the risen Christ we see what humanity will be in God's new creation.

The resurrection of Christ is the beginning of this new creation as the risen Lord has already entered into the fullness of the kingdom he proclaimed. In Jesus' ministry, the kingdom of God made its initial appearance through the mighty works he performed; and in his person the kingdom was already present in a hidden way to those who believed in his message. Although Jesus' death appeared to contradict his proclamation of the kingdom, God brought Jesus into the fullness of the kingdom he proclaimed by raising him from the dead. God's act of raising Jesus from the dead, therefore, was the beginning of a new creation. To be sure, that new creation is still in process since the kingdom of God has not yet come in power and glory for all to see, but for those who believe in the risen Christ the fullness of that new creation is already visible in the resurrection of the one who has entered into the kingdom he proclaimed.

Saint Paul insists that those who are "in Christ" are "a new creation" (2 Cor 5:17) since the risen Christ has already entered into God's new creation by his resurrection from the dead. For Paul, the resurrection of Christ was the beginning of the resurrection of the dead (1 Cor 15:20). Consequently, Paul sees himself and those who believe in Christ as already living in the new age insofar as they are living in the risen Christ. Those who believe in Christ, however, have not yet entered into the fullness of God's new creation because they have not been raised from the dead. But when they are, they will enter into the fullness of God's kingdom.

The resurrection of Christ, then, is not an isolated event that happened only to Christ. It is the beginning of the resurrection of the dead whereby those who are raised in Christ will experience what their Lord has already experienced. This is why the resurrection of Christ is an act of God that brings about a new creation for Christ and his followers.

Resurrection from the dead is a new act of creation. For just as God once called humanity into being, so God calls the dead in Christ into a new creation by raising them to new life. This act of calling humanity into a new creation is an utter act of grace grounded in God's love for creation. God is not "obliged" to give the dead new life. Humanity has not "earned" the right to enter into God's new creation. God calls humanity into this new creation because God sees and loves in humanity what he sees and loves in his own Son. And so having raised Jesus from the dead, God raises those who believe in Jesus from the dead.

This resurrection from the dead, however, is not a mere return to life. Resurrection is a matter of being transformed by the power of God's own Spirit so that those who are raised in Christ are perfectly conformed to their risen Lord. What has happened to Christ will happen to those who believe in him. What the risen Christ has become, those who are raised from the dead will be: a new creation animated and empowered by God's Spirit.

Understood as a new creation, the resurrection of the dead means entrance into the fullness of God's life—eternal life. It is entrance into the heavenly sanctuary, the city of God—God's Sabbath rest, as the Epistle to the Hebrews says. Because it is a new creation, it cannot be understood until it is experienced, and even then it will not be completely comprehended since this new creation is an utterly new relationship with God that will not and cannot end.

## The Resurrection and the Community of the Church

The community of the church is the place where the rest of humanity should be able to see the beginning of God's new creation. To be sure, the church is not always the perfect reflection of what it

ought to be. To be sure, the church often falls short of living according to the new life that God has bestowed upon it in Christ. This said,
it is the church that points to God's new creation made possible by
Jesus' resurrection from the dead.

God called the church into being by raising Jesus from the dead.
The community of Jesus' disciples that had been scattered after his
crucifixion was created anew when the risen Lord commissioned
his disciples to preach the gospel of the kingdom to all the nations
of the world. The resurrection of Jesus released the power of God's
Spirit upon this community, transforming and enabling it to proclaim the kingdom of God.

The church, then, exists because of and for the resurrection. It
exists because God raised Jesus from the dead, and it exists to proclaim the resurrection of the dead. If Jesus had not been raised from
the dead, there would be no church, and if God did not raise Jesus
from the dead, the church would be deprived of his central message:
the kingdom of God that finds its fulfillment in the resurrection of
the dead. Thus there is an intimate bond between the resurrection
of Jesus and the birth and life of the church.

Inasmuch as the church is the body of the crucified and risen
Christ, the church already experiences the victory of its risen Lord.
Those who belong to the church are members of the body of Christ,
each member playing a vital role within the church through the
power of the Spirit released by Christ's resurrection. To live in this
church, then, is to live in the sphere of the risen Christ. To live in the
community of the church is to live with the hope that what Christ
is we will become.

The letters to the Colossians and Ephesians express this theology
of the body of Christ in a different way. They speak of the church as
the "body" of Christ and of Christ as the "head" of the body. This
way of understanding the church enables these letters to describe
believers as already raised up with Christ. For, if the "head" of the
body has been raised up, then the "body" has been raised up, if not
literally, then figuratively.

This is why the sacramental life of the church is so important.
Through the sacraments, especially the sacraments of baptism and

Eucharist, the church participates in the mystery of Christ's resurrection. In baptism believers die with Christ so that they can live in the newness of Christ's resurrection life. In their baptism they are already raised up with Christ in a sacramental way. Participation in the Eucharist provides another way for the church to experience and proclaim the Lord's death and resurrection. Every time the church celebrates the resurrection it proclaims the death of its risen Lord until he comes again (1 Cor 11:26). Every time the church celebrates the Eucharist it participates in the risen life of its Lord (1 Cor 10:16-17).

Finally, because the church is the bride of Christ, it is intimately united with its crucified and risen Lord. The church is the bride of a living person—the risen Christ whom God called into the new creation. The whole purpose of this marriage metaphor is to remind and assure believers of the intimate union that exists between them and their risen Lord.

The community of the church, then, exists because it experiences and witnesses to the resurrection of its Lord as it waits for the general resurrection of the dead. The church exists because God raised Jesus from the dead. Because the church is the body of Christ, it experiences the power of Christ's resurrection in the gift of the Spirit and its sacramental life. Because the church experiences this power, it proclaims the resurrection of the dead to others so that they can experience the resurrection for which the church waits.

## The Resurrection and the Life of the Believer

The individual Christian lives within the community of the church. Since the Christian lives within a community of other believers, the life and identity of the Christian is formed and determined, in large measure, by the community of the church that witnesses to its Lord's resurrection.

People enter into the community of the church because they have come to believe what the church believes and proclaims about the resurrection of Jesus. A person begins to believe at some level that Jesus Christ is risen and alive, that the risen Christ is present in his or her life. Apart from this kind of faith it makes little sense to be a Christian. But when one comes to such faith, one enters the community of believers who proclaim the Lord's resurrection. Put another way, just as the church exists because of and to proclaim the resurrection, so the Christian lives because of and to proclaim the resurrection.

To say that the Christian exists because of the resurrection is to affirm that it is the power of Christ's resurrection that enables the Christian to live within the church community as part of the new creation God is forming in Christ. The Christian already experiences something of Christ's resurrection through the power of the Spirit that comes from the risen Lord.

Prior to becoming Christians, believers lived in the realm of the old Adam. In solidarity with the old Adam, they lived in what Paul calls the realm of the flesh, the realm of what is purely human and turned in on itself. Those who do not live in the realm of the Spirit, Paul says, cannot please God (Rom 8:8). They may know what is right; they may even want to do what is right; they may even do what is right from time to time; but they do not have the inner power to live consistently in a way pleasing to God (Rom 7:7-25). This is why the resurrection of Christ is so important for the Christian—for it is the resurrection that releases the power of the Spirit that empowers Christians to live in a way they were unable to live before.

The resurrection of Christ, then, is not simply an event of the past; it is something that affects those who believe in the risen Lord. The resurrection of Christ releases the power of God's Spirit into the world so that believers already experience something of the resurrection life their Lord has already attained. But there is more. Because believers have received the gift of the Spirit, they already have the promise of eternal life within them: for just as God raised Jesus from the dead by the power of the Spirit, so God will raise from the dead those who possess the gift of the Spirit bestowed by Jesus' resurrection (Rom 8:11).

Those who have experienced the power of Christ's resurrection in their lives understand their destiny—to be raised from the dead just as Christ was raised from the dead. And because they understand the goal and purpose of their lives, they proclaim the gospel of the Lord's resurrection. Thus the experience of and hope for the resurrection impel believers to make disciples of all nations.

The resurrection of Christ is both the origin and goal of the Christian life. It is the origin of the Christian life inasmuch as it calls Christians into being and empowers them to live in a way pleasing to God. It is the goal of the Christian life inasmuch as the destiny of Christ is the destiny of those who believe in him. Just as Christ was taken up into the life of God to participate in God's new creation, so Christians will be taken up into the life of God and enter into the fullness of God's kingdom at the resurrection of the dead.

## The Resurrection as a Mystery of Faith

The resurrection is a mystery of faith. It is not a mystery in the sense that it cannot be known. It is not a mystery in the sense that it can be solved. Rather, it is a mystery in the sense that it must be experienced to be understood, and even then there will always be something new to experience and understand.

In everyday language a mystery refers to something that is puzzling and difficult to understand. But in most instances, such mysteries can be resolved and understood. But this is not the kind of mystery that the resurrection is. The resurrection is an act of God that transcends our human understanding. It is an act of God that goes beyond human understanding. It is an act of God that needs to be experienced.

For example, we proclaim that Jesus Christ has been raised from the dead. We profess that he entered into a totally new sphere of life. But exactly what this means we do not know because we have not yet entered into the fullness of God's kingdom; we have not entered into the fullness of God's new creation. Therefore, it is only at the resurrection of the dead that we will understand what it means to be raised from the dead. When we have experienced what Jesus has experienced, we will understand the new life he already enjoys.

But even then, when we experience the resurrection, the resurrection will remain a mystery, the most sublime and beautiful of all mysteries. For, as we enter into the mystery of the resurrection we enter ever more deeply into the inexhaustible life of God. And the more deeply we enter into the mystery, the more we will understand how little we understand.

How could it be otherwise? How could we ever hope to fathom the depth of God's life? If we could exhaust the mystery, God would not be God. If we could exhaust the mystery, there would be a moment when we would become "bored" with our resurrection life. This is why the resurrection is and remains a mystery that reveals and conceals, a mystery into which we will never cease to enter ever more deeply.

# Annotated Bibliography for Further Reading

Alkier, Stefan. *The Reality of the Resurrection: The New Testament Witness*. Translated by Leroy A. Huizenga. Waco: Baylor University Press, 2013. This historical, canonical, and hermeneutical study attempts to bridge the chasm between history and theology in the discussion of the resurrection.

Bieringer, R., V. Koperski, and B. Lataire, eds. *Resurrection in the New Testament: Festschrift J. Lambrecht*. Bibliotheca Ephemeridum Theologicarum Lovaniensium 165. Leuven: Peeters, 2002. This series of scholarly articles deals with various aspects of the resurrection in the gospels, the Pauline literature, 1 Peter, and the Gospel of Peter.

Bryan, Christopher. *The Resurrection of the Messiah*. New York: Oxford University Press, 2011. This is a very readable volume that begins by exploring how life after death was understood in the ancient world. It then examines the major witnesses to the resurrection in the New Testament. It concludes by asking what we should make of the claims of these witnesses.

Charlesworth, James H., with C. D. Elledge, J. L. Crenshaw, H. Boers, and W. W. Willis Jr. *Resurrection: The Origin and Future of a Biblical Doctrine*. Faith and Scholarship Colloquies Series. New York: T & T Clark, 2006. The authors of this volume explore the background of the concept of resurrection and its meaning for the present day.

Durrwell, F.-X. *The Resurrection: A Biblical Study*. Translated by Rosemary Sheed. New York: Sheed and Ward, 1960. This is a classic work that deserves to be read again. It examines the theological meaning of the resurrection as it is presented in the New Testament.

———. *Christ Our Passover: The Indispensable Role of Resurrection in Our Salvation.* Translated by John F. Craghan. Liguori, MO: Liguori, 2004. This short but rich volume presents the author's mature thought on an issue with which he dealt his whole life long.

Kirk, J. R. Daniel. *Unlocking Romans: Resurrection and the Justification of God.* Grand Rapids: Eerdmans, 2008. This volume shows the centrality of the resurrection in the thought of St. Paul's most important letter.

Moloney, Francis J. *The Resurrection of the Messiah: A Narrative Commentary on the Resurrection Accounts in the Four Gospels.* New York: Paulist Press, 2013. This excellent volume presents the theological dimensions of the gospel resurrection narratives in light of a narrative reading of the text.

O'Collins, Gerald. *Believing in the Resurrection: The Meaning and Promise of the Risen Jesus.* New York: Paulist Press, 2012. This volume presents an insightful apologia for the claims that believers make for the resurrection of Jesus.

Schneiders, Sandra. *Jesus Risen in Our Midst: Essays on the Resurrection of Jesus in the Fourth Gospel.* Collegeville, MN: Liturgical Press, 2013. This series of essays focuses on the distinctive way in which the Fourth Gospel presents the resurrection.

Thiselton, Anthony C. *Life after Death: A New Approach to the Last Things.* Grand Rapids: Eerdmans, 2012. This is a philosophical and theological work that examines the meaning of Christ's resurrection, his second coming, the final judgment, and the beatific vision.

Van Oyen, Geert, and Tom Shepherd, eds. *Resurrection of the Dead: Biblical Traditions in Dialogue.* Bibliotheca Ephemeridum Theologicarum Lovaniensium 249. Leuven: Peeters, 2012. This volume is the fruit of a symposium on the resurrection. It deals with the resurrection in the Old and New Testaments, as well as with the history, theology, and hermeneutics of the resurrection.

Wright, N. T. *The Resurrection of the Son of God.* Christian Origins and the Question of God, vol. 3. Minneapolis: Fortress, 2003. This long but readable work deals with nearly every aspect of the resurrection in the Old and New Testaments. It is the most important work on the resurrection in our time.

# Scripture Index

**Genesis**
49:9     128–29

**Exodus**
3:6     29

**Leviticus**
16     116

**Deuteronomy**
18:15     72
21:23     17n3

**1 Kings**
17:17-24     25

**Psalms**
2:7     114, 115
8     117
16     77
16:8-11     70
95     117
110:1     70, 114
110:4     114, 115
118:22     73

**Daniel**
7:9     128
7:13     127
7:13-14     17n4
7:14     30
7:27     30–31
10:5     127–28
10:6     128
12:2-3     31

**Matthew**
1:23     49
2:11     48
3:17     49
4:23     49
5–7     49
9:35     49
10:6     49
10:8     22–23
11:1     49
11:5     22
14:2     20
14:33     49
15:24     50
16:16     49

16:21     46, 47
17:23     46, 47
18:20     49
20:19     46, 47
21:28     49
24:47     14
26:15     48
26:32     47
27:60-61     47
27:63     33
27:51-53     47
27:52     50
27:54     49
27:62-66     46
27:64-65     48
27:65     46
28:1-10     46
28:7     47
28:8     48
28:9     48
28:10     48
28:11-15     46
28:15     48
28:16-20     9, 46
28:17     46, 48

| | |
|---|---|
| 28:19 | 14, 49, 50 |

**Mark**

| | |
|---|---|
| 1:15 | 4 |
| 5:21-24 | 23 |
| 5:25-34 | 23 |
| 5:35-43 | 23 |
| 6:16 | 20 |
| 8:31 | 30 |
| 8:38 | 33 |
| 9:10 | 32 |
| 9:14-29 | 24–25 |
| 9:31 | 31, 134 |
| 10:33-34 | 31–32 |
| 12:13-17 | 28 |
| 12:18-27 | 28 |
| 12:26-27 | 29 |
| 12:28-34 | 28 |
| 13:26-27 | 33 |
| 14:25 | 33 |
| 14:28 | 33 |
| 14:62 | 33 |
| 14:3-9 | 39–40 |
| 14:27-28 | 40 |
| 14:28 | 8, 41 |
| 15:29-32 | 44 |
| 15:34 | 44 |
| 15:46 | 40 |
| 15:40, 47 | 39, 43 |
| 16:1-8 | 38–39, 40, 42, 43, 44, 46, 51, 62n6 |
| 16:4 | 135 |
| 16:7 | 8, 33 |
| 16:9-20 | 42, 43, 62n6 |
| 16:12-13 | 52 |

**Luke**

| | |
|---|---|
| 1:3-4 | 65 |
| 1:68 | 25 |
| 1:78 | 25 |
| 2:46 | 20 |
| 7:11-17 | 25 |
| 7:22 | 22, 25–26 |
| 8:3 | 52 |
| 8:36-50 | 63n11 |
| 9:16 | 53 |
| 9:22 | 32 |
| 9:31 | 55 |
| 9:44 | 52 |
| 9:45 | 53 |
| 9:51 | 55, 63n10 |
| 12:11-12 | 72–73 |
| 17:22-37 | 33 |
| 18:33 | 32 |
| 20:2 | 72 |
| 20:34-36 | 29 |
| 22:19-23 | 53 |
| 23:47 | 25 |
| 24:1-12 | 51 |
| 24:10 | 52 |
| 24:13-35 | 51 |
| 24:16 | 53 |
| 24:19 | 53 |
| 24:26-48 | 9 |
| 24:27 | 58 |
| 24:34 | 53 |
| 24:36-49 | 51 |
| 24:45 | 54 |
| 24:46 | 69 |
| 24:46-48 | 54–55, 58 |
| 24:49 | 69 |
| 24:50-53 | 51 |

**John**

| | |
|---|---|
| 1:19, 36 | 129 |
| 1:19–12:50 | 26 |
| 1:29 | 58 |
| 2:19 | 21 |
| 2:21-22 | 21 |
| 4:25-26 | 125 |
| 5:21 | 22, 27, 124 |
| 5:28-29 | 22 |
| 6:54 | 10, 124 |
| 7:34 | 21 |
| 7:35 | 21 |
| 8:21 | 21 |
| 10:17-18 | 22 |
| 10:3-5 | 57 |
| 11:21-26 | 26–27 |
| 11:45-53 | 26 |
| 14:2-3, 19, 28 | 21 |
| 16:5, 16 | 21 |
| 16:28 | 21 |
| 17:3 | 125 |
| 20:1-18 | 56 |
| 20:8 | 57 |
| 20:9 | 57 |
| 20:18 | 57 |
| 20:19 | 58 |
| 20:19-23 | 56 |
| 20:21 | 58 |
| 20:24 | 58 |
| 20:24-29 | 56 |
| 20:25 | 9 |
| 20:29 | 58 |
| 20:30-31 | 56, 59 |
| 21:1 | 59 |
| 21:1-14 | 59 |
| 21:1-19 | 56 |
| 21:15-19 | 9, 59 |

| | | | | | | |
|---|---|---|---|---|---|---|
| 21:20 | 59 | 13:32-33 | 77 | 4:17 | 90 |
| 21:20-23 | 59 | 13:35 | 77 | 4:23-25 | 90 |
| 21:20-25 | 56 | 13:38-39 | 77 | 4:24-25 | 11–12 |
| 21:22 | 59–60 | 17:2-3 | 78 | 4:25 | 91 |
| | | 17:22-31 | 78–79 | 5:12 | 11 |
| **Acts** | | 17:18 | 78 | 6 | 105 |
| 1:3 | 14, 66 | 17:22-28 | 78 | 6:1-4 | 103 |
| 1:4 | 69 | 17:29-31 | 78 | 6:4 | 10 |
| 1:8 | 9, 14, 66 | 17:31 | 79 | 6:5 | 104 |
| 1:21-22 | 66 | 17:32 | 79 | 6:8 | 104 |
| 2:14-21 | 69 | 21:28 | 80 | 7:7-25 | 140 |
| 2:14-36 | 69 | 22 | 67, 86 | 8:8 | 104, 140 |
| 2:22-24 | 69 | 22:1-21 | 79, 80 | 8:9 | 97, 101 |
| 2:23-24 | 4, 135 | 22:6 | 67, 87 | 8:11 | 6, 97, 140 |
| 2:25-36 | 70 | 22:8 | 67 | 8:14-17 | 97 |
| 2:32-33 | 6 | 22:12 | 67 | 8:18-21 | 13 |
| 2:33 | 67 | 22:14, 15 | 67–68 | 8:18-23 | 109 |
| 2:36 | 70–71 | 22:17-21 | 68 | 8:23 | 97–98 |
| 3:1-10 | 71 | 23:6 | 79, 8 | 8:29-30 | 109–10 |
| 3:11-16 | 71 | 23:8 | 28 | 8:34 | 91 |
| 3:17-26 | 71 | 24:5-6, 12 | 80 | 8:38-39 | 135 |
| 4:2 | 72 | 24:10-21 | 79–80 | 9:24 | 99 |
| 4:8 | 72 | 24:15 | 80 | 10:4 | 85 |
| 4:11 | 73 | 24:21 | 80 | 12:4-5 | 100 |
| 4:18 | 73 | 26 | 67, 86 | 12:5 | 102 |
| 4:19-20 | 73 | 26:2-23 | 80, 81 | | |
| 5:29-32 | 73 | 26:6-7 | 81 | **1 Corinthians** | |
| 9 | 67, 86 | 26:6-8 | 7 | 1:1 | 87 |
| 9:3 | 87 | 26:8 | 81 | 1:2 | 99 |
| 9:4 | 67 | 26:13 | 68, 87 | 2:1 | 85 |
| 9:5 | 67 | 26:14 | 68 | 3:16-17 | 100 |
| 9:15 | 65 | 26:16-18 | 68 | 6:17 | 101 |
| 9:20, 22 | 67 | 26:22-23 | 81 | 10:16-17 | 139 |
| 10:1–11:18 | 74–75 | | | 11:23 | 87 |
| 10:34-43 | 74 | **Romans** | | 11:26 | 139 |
| 13:16-41 | 76–78 | 1:1 | 87 | 12:27 | 100, 102 |
| 13:17-25 | 76 | 1:3-4 | 90 | 15 | 29, 57 |
| 13:26-41 | 76 | 1:4 | 99 | 15:1-11 | 94 |
| 13:30 | 76 | 3:25 | 99 | 15:3 | 87 |

| | | | | | | |
|---|---|---|---|---|---|
| 15:3-5 | 88, 89, 134 | 1:10 | 85 | 2:11-12 | 93 |
| 15:6-9 | 89 | 1:11 | 99 | **Titus** | |
| 15:8 | 86 | 1:14 | 98 | 3:4-7 | 98 |
| 15:12-28 | 94 | 1:19-23 | 135 | | |
| 15:17 | 85 | 1:22-23 | 101 | **Hebrews** | |
| 15:19 | 13 | 2:4-6 | 102, 106 | 1:3 | 114, 132n2 |
| 15:20 | 136 | 2:19-22 | 100 | 1:5-13 | 114–15 |
| 15:22-28 | 108 | 4:15-16 | 101 | 1:6 | 118 |
| 15:23 | 94 | 4:30 | 6, 98 | 2:5-9 | 117 |
| 15:35-58 | 94–96 | 5:14 | 92 | 2:9 | 136 |
| 15:35-44 | 94–95 | | | 2:10 | 113, 116–17 |
| 15:45-49 | 95 | **Philippians** | | 3:7–4:7 | 117 |
| 15:50-57 | 96 | 2:5-11 | 91–92 | 4:8-11 | 117 |
| | | 3:20-21 | 95, 108 | 5:5 | 115 |
| **2 Corinthians** | | 3:21 | 126 | 5:9 | 117 |
| 1:22 | 6, 98 | | | 6:1-2 | 113 |
| 3:18 | 87, 110 | **Colossians** | | 7:23-25 | 115 |
| 4:3, 6 | 87 | 1:1 | 87 | 7:25 | 116 |
| 4:6 | 85 | 1:15-20 | 91, 92 | 9:11-12 | 116 |
| 4:12-14 | 107–8 | 1:18 | 5, 101, 102 | 10:12 | 116 |
| 5:1-10 | 96 | 2:12 | 102 | 11:10 | 118 |
| 5:16 | 85 | 2:12-13 | 105 | 11:16 | 118 |
| 5:17 | 136 | 3:1-3 | 12 | 11:19 | 118 |
| | | 3:1-4 | 105 | 11:35 | 118 |
| **Galatians** | | 3:5 | 106 | 12:2 | 116 |
| 1–2 | 86 | 3:10 | 106 | 12:22-24 | 118 |
| 1:12 | 86 | | | 13:20 | 113 |
| 1:13-14 | 86 | **1 Thessalonians** | | | |
| 1:15-16 | 14 | 1:9-10 | 79 | **1 Peter** | |
| 1:15-17 | 86 | 1:9-10 | 89 | 1:3 | 122 |
| 2:16 | 86 | 4:13-14 | 107 | 1:3–2:10 | 122 |
| 3:5 | 6 | 4:14 | 89 | 1:4-5 | 122 |
| 3:13 | 17n3, 85 | | | 1:11 | 120 |
| 5:19 | 104 | **1 Timothy** | | 1:20-21 | 120 |
| 5:22-23 | 104 | 3:16 | 92–93 | 1:23 | 122 |
| | | | | 2:2 | 122 |
| **Ephesians** | | **2 Timothy** | | | |
| 1:7-10 | 110 | 1:1 | 87 | | |

| | | | | | |
|---|---|---|---|---|---|
| 2:5 | 122 | 3:14 | 124 | 2:11 | 128 |
| 2:10 | 122 | 3:16 | 124 | 2:12 | 128 |
| 2:11–4:11 | 122 | 4:2 | 125 | 2:17 | 128 |
| 2:21-25 | 120–21 | 4:7 | 125 | 2:18 | 128 |
| 3:13-14 | 121 | 5:1 | 125 | 2:26 | 128 |
| 3:18-22 | 121 | 5:4 | 125 | 3:5 | 128 |
| 3:21 | 122 | 5:11-12 | 124 | 3:12 | 128 |
| 5:1 | 122–23 | 5:20 | 124 | 3:21 | 128 |
| | | | | 5:5-6 | 128 |
| **2 Peter** | | **Revelation** | | 5:9-10 | 129 |
| 3:13 | 13 | 1:5 | 131 | 5:12 | 129 |
| | | 1:12-16 | 127–28 | 5:13 | 129 |
| **1 John** | | 1:17-18 | 128 | 6:9 | 130 |
| 1:1-2 | 124 | 1:18 | 131 | 6:11 | 130 |
| 2:22-23 | 125 | 2:1 | 128 | 7:1-8 | 130 |
| 2:24-25 | 124 | 2:7 | 128 | 7:9-17 | 130 |
| 3:2-3 | 126 | 2:8 | 128 | 14:1-4 | 130 |
| 3:9 | 125 | 2:10 | 131 | 20:5, 12-13 | 130 |